Hope Begins
Where Hope Begins

Hope Begins
Where Hope Begins

Michael Downey

ORBIS BOOKS

Maryknoll, New York 10545

Published by Orbis Books, Maryknoll, NY 10545-0308
Manufactured in the United States of America

About the cover art:
Los Angeles artist John August Swanson is noted for his finely detailed, brilliantly colored biblical pieces. His works are found in the Smithsonian Institution's National Museum of American History, London's Tate Gallery, the Vatican Museum's Collection of Modern Religious Art, and the Bibliothèque Nationale, Paris. He is represented by the Bergsma Gallery, Grand Rapids, Michigan (616-458-1776). Full-color posters and cards of Mr. Swanson's work are available from the National Association for Hispanic Elderly. Benefits go to its programs of employment of seniors, and to housing low-income seniors. For information, contact the National Association for Hispanic Elderly, 234 East Colorado Boulevard, Suite 300, Pasadena CA 91101 (213-487-1922).

ISBN 1-57075-185-4

Dedicated to my nephews
Richard William Vogel, III
Michael Francis Lamb, Jr.
Reasons to hope
in the next generation,
and the next

Contents

Acknowledgments 9

Introduction: Why Hope? 11

ONE 17
    Beneath Mary's Mantle   18
    Where We Stand   25

TWO 37
    Walking Free   38
    Going Through the Motions   42
    Where Is God Today?   45

THREE 57
    The Talk in Tinsel Town   58
    What Is Hope?   63

FOUR 77
    And They Lived   78
    The Rebirth of Hope:
        Making Room for the Other   83

FIVE 93
    Speaking of Tongues   94
    Christ: The Ground of Hope   104

SIX 113
    Doxology in Darkness   114
    Conclusion   125

Acknowledgments

I am delighted to acknowledge here my gratitude for the opportunity to hold the Flannery Endowed Chair of Roman Catholic Theology at Gonzaga University in Spokane, Washington, during the 1996–97 academic year. It was in the course of my reading in preparation for the Flannery Lecture on March 4, 1997, that I was able to bring together my thoughts on hope.

Part of the virtue of hope is patient waiting for what is yet to come. Susan Perry, my editor at Orbis Books, has emerged as a paragon of this virtue as one interruption and then another caused yet further delay in my making good on a promise. I am deeply grateful for her commitment to this book, and for her painstaking editorial skill. I would also like to thank Robert Ellsberg, editor-in-chief at Orbis.

The Benedictine community of the Monastery of Saint Gertrude in Cottonwood, Idaho, offered me hospitality and the solitude necessary to bring this work to completion.

Finally, I acknowledge my enduring gratitude to my brothers at Mepkin Abbey in South Carolina, who have given me yet another reason to hope.

MICHAEL EDWARD DOWNEY

19 October 1997
Thérèse of Lisieux proclaimed
  Doctor of the Church
The "Little Doctor of Hope"

Introduction

Why Hope?

*Always have your answer ready for people who
ask you the reason for the hope that you have.*

(1 Peter 3:15)

In every age, in each culture, Christians have been called upon to give an account of why they hope. In an age such as ours, one marked by massive and meaningless death, not just of individuals but of whole peoples and cultures, Christians must be prepared to explain the nature of their hope, specifically hope in Jesus Christ, the hope of all. This is the challenge I have set for myself in this small book.

Upon hearing that I was writing a book on hope, an astonishing number of people remarked: "Good. We need it. We need hope as never before." In my research and in my writing I have been buoyed up over and over again by encouraging words such as these, but I have wondered again and again just what sort of book would be helpful to those who recognize the need for hope as something very deep within each of us.

These pages are the result of pondering over several simple questions:

- Why does hope seem so hard to come by in our own day and age?

- Just what is hope?

- What are the conditions necessary for hope, and how is hope retrieved once it has been lost?

- What does it mean to say that we hope in Christ, and that Christ is the ground of our hope?

In wrestling with these questions over the last few years, I have come to understand a little about hope. What I have learned might be of some help to others who are looking for a reason to hope.

Why hope? Why a book on hope? And why have I written a book on hope? I am sure that I am not alone in noticing the general mood of despondency in our time. There is a sort of all-pervasive cynicism toward government, authority, and religion — a skepticism in the face of anyone or anything that would make a binding claim upon us. Many people have been deeply wounded by institutions and systems that day by day seem to become more impersonal and depersonalizing. Patients in some hospitals and medical centers are now referred to as customers. In some instances these customers are called consumers. But the human person, especially when vulnerable and fragile because of handicap, accident, illness, or old age, is much more than a consumer to be "serviced" by a "health care provider." Some people know in their marrow that there is something quite wrong with this way of relating to one another. It causes a deep ache in the soul. But many are at a loss to know what to do about it. It continues to haunt and hurt.

In addition to the somber mood of the world in which we live, it is hard not to note the increasing number of people suffering from depression. Though depression is nothing new and there have always been people who have suffered from this form of mental disorder, it seems beyond dispute that the number of those diagnosed with depression and seeking help has simply skyrocketed in recent years.

Both the mood of despondency and the sharp rise in the number of people who suffer from depression make me wonder if there is a relationship between these factors and the reality of hope. Has our culture of individualism, pragmatism, and restlessness brought a dark mood over the whole land, resulting in so many of our young taking their own lives? Why are there so many who appear to hope only for the preservation of their own individual rights and liberties, or for more "things," for greater upward mobility? Are there other reasons for the listlessness, the sag of the human spirit that seems to have become commonplace? Is there a deeper reason for that long tired sigh, that wide yawn, at the very sight or sound of anything other than what seem to be the two consuming preoccupations of people in the United States: sports and business (or is it sex)?

Aside from the general despondency of a whole people, there is also the despondency of particular persons. In-

deed, many of them. This may be brought on by many
factors: genetic inheritance, severe stress, trauma, or personal loss. And loss takes many forms. We may lose a
parent, child, friend, good health, reputation, home, work.
Often this personal despondency or depression results in
a darkness so intolerable that death may seem prefer-
able. What is the relationship between hope and this deep
darkness of soul, mind, and body called depression?

These are the questions that lie at the core of this little
book. In struggling with these questions, I am writing
from two firm convictions. First, there is nothing more
central to being human than being able to hope. And, second, hope of the deepest kind can come only as a gift
from God.

When I was thinking about how to write this book
and whom I was writing for, I decided to combine stories
and some poetry with the text. Stories and poetry create
images and give hints or clues about ultimate questions
and meanings, perhaps a trace of what we are searching for. Oftentimes stories draw us in somehow, while
teachings that systematize or try to provide a complete
or total explanation may leave us untouched. Stories are
often the link that moves us from emotions and feelings
to concepts. While emotions stir us and make us think,
concepts give us a framework for understanding. Understanding and, in particular, understanding the shape of
our life with God can lead us toward hope.

The Old Testament is replete with images of hope.
Los Angeles artist John August Swanson's *Dream of Ja-*

cob (Genesis 28:10ff), which graces the cover of this book, evokes hope from deep within the human heart. Jacob sleeps in a deep green valley, reminiscent perhaps of the psalmist's dark valley of death (Psalm 23). Stretched out under a million stars atwinkle in a midnight-blue sky, Jacob is relaxed, receptive, vulnerable as we all are in our sleep. Even though it may appear that nothing is going on because he is asleep, something wonderful is at work: Jacob is being offered a future possibility that comes only as a gift. The eye first catches sleeping Jacob, seemingly swallowed in the darkness of lush greens and blues. Gradually the eye begins to rest on the shaft of light that comes from elsewhere, from above or beyond. The eye follows it — onward and upward. Wherever the light's origin or destination may be, it is neither of Jacob's own making, nor the result of his own efforts. The light encircling the ladder pierces the darkness of the night, offering a glimpse of a way and a world that Jacob can only dream about, imagine, hope for. Those who would receive the gift being offered, even winged angels, must climb the ladder rung by rung, step by step. Only by so doing can we move toward the fulfillment of what has been promised.

I chose the title of this book after a conversation with Jon Sobrino, a Jesuit theologian who lives and works with the poor in El Salvador. In discussing the dynamics of hope during a meeting of theologians in New York City in 1995, Sobrino seemed at a loss to explain how it is that many of the poor go on in the face of seemingly insurmountable obstacles, while others who shoulder a comparatively lighter burden simply do not or cannot. Much to the dismay of many gathered there, he concluded with the simple observation: "Hope begins where hope begins." Sobrino's words seem to express that great mystery at the core of human freedom and responsibility, that mystery we name hope. Without it we do not live. Indeed, wherever there is life there is hope. Traces of it are found each time we take the next step. Because of its light we turn the page and we are able to look from one moment to the next. It looks to a future that can come only as gift. It begins where it begins. And hope, the deep-down kind, has no end. It is like faith. It is no less than love.

O N E

And indeed everything that was written long ago in the scriptures was meant to teach us something about hope . . . of how people who did not give up were helped by God.

(Romans 15:4)

Beneath Mary's Mantle

"It's gone." I could hear her voice in the parking lot. "That's a blue car. But it's not mine. Where's *my* car? My car's gone." We stood on the steps of the rectory in utter disbelief.

Pentecost Sunday, June 4, 1995, 4:45 P.M. Broad daylight. This is a private parking lot in front of a rectory near the National Shrine of the Immaculate Conception. Dedicated to Our Lady. The car doors are all locked. Nothing on view inside the car. And *everything* locked in the trunk of the car! Gone.

Mother and I thought it would be nice to bring cousin Maria for a tour of Washington, D.C. I had persuaded her to come to the United States for a vacation with us. She works as a nurse's aide in Dublin, and she had saved for a year so that she could afford the trip. She was born and raised in Clones, a town that sits right smack-dab on the border of Ireland and Northern Ireland, during the "troubles," the conflict between Catholics and Protestants, so she has never known a time of peace on her native soil.

This would be her first visit to America. And what would a trip to the U.S.A. be like without a visit to our nation's capital? So we set out from Philadelphia in Mother's car for an overnight trip.

We stayed with some friends living just outside D.C. I've known them since the days when I was active in the Charismatic Renewal as a student in Washington. The weather was absolutely perfect. And how appropriate, I thought, to go to Mass on Pentecost Sunday with these dear friends from the days of my involvement with the charismatics. After Mass there was a lovely brunch back at their home served by Elizabeth, Dennis and Jeannie's thirteen-year-old daughter. Just prior to departure we loaded the trunk of Mother's car. Seven-year-old David, my godson, wanted to come with us. The rest of the family had plans to go to a picnic for the rest of the day, so we agreed that we would take David with us and drop him off at the picnic later, after making a quick tour of Washington.

We wanted Maria to get a glimpse of all the sights: the monuments, White House, Pentagon, Capitol Building, Arlington Cemetery. But we didn't plan to do the whole town. I know that tourists are easy prey in D.C. I'm always a bit on edge in that town, having been robbed at knife point in the late 1970s and having had my apartment vandalized and looted more times than I care to tell.

In the afternoon, on our way to drop off David with his family, I thought we might make a quick stop to visit

a priest, a friend Mother had not seen in a long time.
Since he's Irish, I thought it might be a treat for both him
and cousin Maria. I stopped to phone, telling him that we
would arrive in twenty minutes. He was waiting at the
front door at 4:30, just as planned.

We sat in the rectory parlor that overlooks the parking
lot in front of the rectory. Chatting it up, our attention
was fixed on one another and the lighthearted conversation. I was aware of time passing since I wanted to complete the three-hour drive to Philadelphia before nightfall.
We declined even a cup of tea. At 4:45 I hastened my trav-
eling companions to the door. After kisses and hugs all
around, we descended the stairs. "It's gone."

I had been even more cautious than usual to assure that
all four doors of the car were locked. I had my mother, a
"foreigner," and my godchild. And since I know that maps
and souvenirs on view can be a dead giveaway, I was careful not to leave any such clues in sight. Everything was
securely locked in the trunk. We just wanted to "stop in
for a minute or two." I had actually considered hauling
the whole trunkful into the rectory for our fifteen-minute
visit. Experience had taught me to be very careful.

The car had been stolen within fifteen minutes, from a
private parking lot in front of a rectory, in broad daylight,
in the shadow of Our Lady's Shrine! Right from beneath
Mary's mantle: Maria's passport, traveler's checks, cash,
several airplane tickets, suitcases jammed with clothing,
souvenirs, and all those little things that you count on
day in and day out. The whole lot. Those address books

with telephone numbers accumulated over the last God-knows-how-many-years. Appointment calendars that remind you where you should be next week. And next month. And next year. Then there were printouts of three lectures I was scheduled to give in different parts of the country throughout June. And the notes for a retreat I was scheduled to lead at the end of the month. We stood there with nothing but the clothes we were wearing. I had a wallet and comb in my back pocket. David said something about wanting to go to the picnic.

That, of course, was only the beginning. We did everything we were supposed to do: called 911, filed police reports, telephoned insurance agencies. Some people seemed somewhat startled, as we told the story again and again and again. But no one in Washington seemed quite as shocked as we were. It seems this sort of thing happens every day. We were told right off the bat that we should not expect to see the car again. "D.C.'s broke. We're outta money. So we don't go looking for stolen cars. We'll call you if it turns up," reported Officer McBride. I took her at her word.

My losses seemed minor by comparison. Mother's car was gone, with lots of her personal belongings. And Maria. Poor Maria had saved all year long to make the trip. She had bought all new clothes. She'd been accumulating souvenirs for family and friends. All gone.

Our priest friend drove us back to Dennis and Jeannie's. Their house had always seemed like a haven to me. A real home. It was all that and more on that Pentecost

Sunday. We were quickly reminded that we should count our blessings that no one was hurt. These weren't just empty words, but at the time they were hardly a cause for rejoicing.

Dennis helped me take one step at a time. Jeannie looked after Mother and Maria. Opening up his wardrobe, Dennis told me to take what I needed. Jeannie gave Maria what she needed to get her through the next few days. We rented a car, and then went the next morning to the Irish Embassy to replace Maria's passport. Then on to the drugstore to replace medication that Mother needed badly. We took turns calling insurance companies and police headquarters, and canceling appointments. And then we began to pay fees. For stolen airplane tickets, for example. I learned that the airline companies have no box to check for "stolen" tickets. Only "lost," which, of course, makes you feel that it's your forgetfulness or stupidity or absent-mindedness that has put you in this position.

A small thing, right? And no one was physically hurt. No major catastrophe, to be sure. And so it was hard for many ostensibly sympathetic listeners to wrap their minds around the sense of profound disorientation that this little episode caused us. That's the point. It's the little things like this that interrupt our lives, disorient us profoundly. We are overwhelmed. And it happens time and again.

The event of Pentecost '95 put a chink in our summer. Everything had to be rescheduled so as to attend to the million little details that kept popping up. And the never-ending paperwork drove us crazy. "We cannot provide a copy of the police report for your insurance company. You will have to wait ninety days. D.C. has no money, and we have a backlog of requests." And then there was the lunacy of the insurance adjuster who would not accept our claim form until thirty days after the incident: "A car isn't stolen unless it's gone for thirty days." I heard it with my own ears!

I doubt Maria will ever return to the U.S. I was grateful that worse had not befallen her. It was hard enough to send her back to her parents with a plastic bag full of jeans and blouses, underwear and pantyhose all marked "Made with pride in the U.S.A." And nothing else.

It's not so much the sense of violation that overcomes you when something like this happens, though there is that. It's more an overwhelming feeling that your living has been interrupted. Your life has been broken into. It's as if you have to start from scratch. All plans must be put on hold. You can't and don't take anything for granted. You rely on the goodness of others, wherever and whenever it might be found. And then you become aware, but only gradually, that the addresses and phone numbers of friends from over the years and across the miles are gone. Then you realize there is not a trace of the lectures you are scheduled to give in five days or of your notes for a retreat for priests the following week. Or of that little memento your friend gave you before he died. The one you always carried in your briefcase so you'd remember him.

And now some strange thief has a key to your house and to your office. And the suitcase in the trunk was the last gift from your parents. The memories are more important than the things themselves.

We managed to find a way together. Eventually the pieces of our lives fell back into place. Mother got a new car. Maria got back to Ireland safely. And I managed to reconstruct those lectures and to lean on the Holy Spirit when leading the retreat. We all managed to keep going, somehow.

We never did see that car or its contents again. I doubt we ever will. When I look back on the episode that threw the summer of '95 into a somersault, I am reminded of how none of our lives seem to unfold according to plan. The stories of our lives begin to sound like a long litany of interruptions and disorientations. Episodes that we would sometimes rather forget. But we cannot and should not. It is in these ruptures and cracks caused by the events that boggle and baffle us that we might see glimmers of hope and a future where we thought there could be none at all. Like the gesture of a friend who opens a wardrobe and says, "Just take what you need." Or in the words of a mother who had suffered more profound losses than this who says confidently, "The car and everything in it can be replaced. Thank God no one was hurt, especially little David." And in the way members of a family brought together from different parts of the globe all counted the other's loss greater than their own.

"The Irish are known for their hospitality," Maria remarked in the days after, "but your friends took me in, a perfect stranger. They were so good to me. They have more hospitality than a lot of the Irish I know. I guess that's because they're Christian. They're really Christians, aren't they? I mean not just Catholics, but Christians."

Where We Stand

These days it is quite common to hear people express the feeling that their lives seem to be coming apart at the seams. The world seems not just hectic but chaotic. What happens in the lives of people and of whole groups of people appears to be random, without any real sense of purpose. A world that once seemed to be orderly and harmonious, though not without pain and suffering and inequity, now looks like a shambles. Is there any longer a unifying meaning or purpose, a value by which people can live? Can the center hold? Is there a future we can look forward to with some measure of confidence?

At the root of questions such as these is the question of hope. In today's world the loss of hope can appear to be so all-pervasive at times that it is difficult to know how to begin to describe it. Or where to begin. Indeed, there is no clear-cut explanation for the loss of something so central to human life.

Yet, somehow, traces of hope still remain in our lives. And signs of hope are visible in the lives of some of those around us. Glimmers of hope may be seen in those few persons who appear to shimmer with radiance as they make their way through life even when everything seems lost, even when there seems to be no reason to go on. Some might refer to such people as modern-day saints. Why? Above all it is because they demonstrate that it is possible to make good on the one and only life each of us has to live. They give us hope because they go on hoping. But why do these people have hope when the rest of us, or at least some of us, don't?

New spiritual gurus of all sorts abound, offering different solutions for filling the void felt by so many. Whether any one of these representatives of the new spiritual quest is on sure footing is arguable. But what seems beyond dispute is that great numbers of people today recognize that even though we have a glut of material things, too much "stuff," we are still deeply dissatisfied. There is an ache of absence. Many of our young, and the not-so-young, wander aimlessly, without direction, without a clear sense of commitment to building a better future, without hope.

Why the hollow feeling? Why do so many look like lost souls? Why are so many places of worship empty? Why is there such a craving for "spirituality" and so little interest in and, indeed, outright hostility toward religion and the church? Although often relegated to lofty academic circles, current discussions about living in a "*post*modern" world may help explain the mood of the world in which we live, a world in which hope seems to be in short supply.

A Postmodern World

It is no longer all that unusual to hear that we are living in a period of history past the "modern" age. Hence, we are past-modern — or "postmodern." The very term "postmodern" is disorienting, jarring. Many find the term odd, and chuckle at the very sound of it, because in common usage "modern" is synonymous with "contemporary." So how can we be past or post *now*? In everyday speech, most of us would say that the microwave oven is a modern way of cooking or that modern technology makes it possible to send quick communiques via fax and e-mail. But the terms "modern" and "postmodern" mean something quite different when they are used to describe different ways of looking at the world, contrasting mind-sets, or distinct historical periods.

"Modern" in this sense refers to a specific period of history, beginning in the eighteenth century with the Age of the Enlightenment, and the work of two European philosophers, René Descartes and Immanuel Kant. This modern period is marked by a particular view of human life, the world, and God.

There are four central features of the modern period or modernity. First, there is *rationalism,* a boundless confidence in the capacity of the human mind to know everything by means of the scientific method. Second,

there is a *dualism* in which one thing is better than
another: God over human beings, humans over nature,
mind over matter, power over weakness, rich over poor,
master over slave, white over colored, clergy over lay,
male over female, intellect over affect, prose over poetry.
Third, there is unbounded confidence in the ability of
the individual to make and shape him- or herself. This
is accompanied by an unprecedented *affirmation of individual rights and liberties,* often to the point where the
common good is abandoned. The fourth feature of the
modern world is its view of *history as inevitably progressive.* Change is improvement, and whatever is new
is better. Progress is inevitable. Whatever can be done
must be done. In such a view the horrors of history and
the sufferings of persons and whole peoples, no matter
how large or atrocious, are seen as just wrinkles in the
unfolding of a future that is thought to be necessarily
better.

Today there is a growing disillusionment with this way
of looking at the world. While ordinary people may not
describe themselves or their world as postmodern, they
often have the nagging sense that there is something quite
wrong with the way of perceiving and being in the world
called "modern." They know in their bones that the mood
created by such a mind-set is fundamentally at odds with
values they hold dear.

The term "postmodern" is itself new and quite am-
biguous. It is used by architects, poets, philosophers,
economists, and now theologians to describe how the cur-

rent cultural, religious, and political climate is different
from that of the modern period. "Postmodern" is a way
of naming the growing sense that the way we have done
it until now is not working, and that we've got to get
past the mess of our own making. Where should we go?
Toward what should we move? The answer is not at all
clear. We seem to be stuck and no one quite knows how
to move into the future or what the future requires of us.
Further, we tend to be highly suspicious of anyone who
would tell us exactly what the creation of a brighter future
demands.

In a scene from a Franz Kafka novel, one traveler
stops another along the road and asks where the other is
headed. The reply of the second traveler: "I don't know.
Only away from here. Only by so doing can I reach my
destination." In this encounter, the second traveler ar-
ticulates what many people feel today. In such a view
there is a widening crack, a fault line growing wider and
wider just beneath the surface of the modern world. If we
are to survive, indeed, if we stand a chance to flourish,
we must move past many of the central convictions of
modernity, that worldview spawned by the Enlightenment
of the eighteenth century.

Perhaps we must leave behind the modern world's notion of history as inevitably progressive. We can see how
the emphasis on individual rights has damaged a sense of
community, how nonhuman forms of life and the earth's
resources have become commodities. We also see the
disastrous consequences of war, hunger and disease for

human beings and for the whole world. We know we must move on. We have to get "away from here." Any place is better.

Viewing the Human Person

Despite the amount of attention given to human beings in the modern era, it is slowly being realized that we have not achieved a deep understanding of the human person or of the social order. The advances of technology have not brought progress and prosperity to the world as promised and, in fact, some of these "advances," such as the availability of atomic or nuclear energy, have caused untold damage. What actually goes on in history, the story of millions of poor and suffering people at the margins or on the underside of society and church, defies explanation.

The modern view of the human person emphasizes the superiority of reason, autonomy, and self-determination. This is quite different from understandings of earlier periods, referred to loosely as "premodern." Before the onset of the modern age, the human person was viewed as more unified. In the thirteenth century, Saint Thomas Aquinas understood the human being as having three distinct capacities: intellect, will, and emotion. Happiness came about through the proper use of these capacities, and intellect and will, mind and heart were not seen as competing with one another. This came about later on, beginning in the eighteenth century. At the risk of oversimplification, we can say that the premodern view of the human person was more integrated and holistic, more appreciative of the importance of relationships and inter-dependence. The meaning and purpose of human life and personal identity were found primarily in rightly ordered relationships with self, others, and God. Personal fulfill-ment was based on recognizing one's place in a clearly ordered world. There was also a strong sense of the coher-ence and meaning of the world. Tragedies and sufferings were accepted as part of God's providential plan, mere wrinkles in the unfolding of a divine tableau. Everything had its place and everyone a purpose within the "big picture." In premodern times God was in charge.

The emphasis on individuality and the superiority of reason came later and eclipsed many of these holistic understandings of the human. Today, some of the cen-tral features of these more holistic views of the human being are welcomed as they seem to correct modernity's bold assertions of autonomy and self-determination, of a world constantly improving because of human initia-tive and understanding. Our postmodern climate today reminds us, once again, that the human person is a re-lational being who is from others, toward others, and for others. Each of us *needs* others.

Interruption

Today our sense of history and of the world is colored by an awareness of interruption and randomness. It seems hard at times to perceive any cohesion or coherence in the world about us. This is brought on by what we have seen in history, by the horror of human suffering and the magnitude of human arrogance that elude the grasp of reason. The Holocaust, Hiroshima, Nagasaki, the American involvement in Vietnam, and genocide in Rwanda and Bosnia have all had a hand in destroying any myths of human progress or explanations of God's providence. When we look at historical events like the American involvement in Vietnam, how can we continue to believe in history as inevitably progressive? Or, how can we attribute such horrors as the Holocaust of the Jews and six million others, or the massacres in Rwanda or Bosnia, to the order of divine providence or to God's permissive will?

Today, things do not always hold together or make sense; there is no longer a unified and unifying worldview that binds and keeps us together. There seems to be no comprehensive, central story either of human progress or of God's presence in and to the world. And there is no one religion or philosophy that adequately explains God's relationship to the world in light of the atrocities of history and the enormity of human suffering caused by the inhumanity of people, ordinary people like us. It is not surprising that many people have no clear sense of the future, no ability to imagine a better and brighter world. Many young people question whether the future will in fact be brighter. Some wonder if they will have a future at all; they cannot imagine a future that they will be able to depend on.

Yet, the way in which history interrupts what we are

doing, the way suffering disorients and baffles us, the difference between what we hope for and what actually happens — all these events make us vulnerable, open to epiphanies, to sudden understandings of what is true. Although it seems at times that there is no "big picture," we can treasure these clues, hints of meaning, snippets of insight. It is often the writer, the artist, or the poet who best speaks of the clues, hints of hope in this age marked by an all-pervasive sense that there are no true maps for our future. Faint traces of hope and the future may be discerned in the lines of the poet Denise Levertov:

> These days — these years —
> when powers and principalities of death
> weigh down the world, deeper, deeper,
> than we ever thought it could fall and still
>   keep slowly spinning.
>
> Hope, caught under the jar's rim, crawls
> like a golden fly
> round and around, a sentinel:
> it can't get out, it can't fly-free
> among our heavy hearts —
> but does not die, keeps up its pace,
> pausing only as if to meditate
> a saving strategy.[1]

---

1. "From the Image-Flow — Summer of 1986," *Breathing the Water* (New York: New Directions, 1984), 41.

And rays of hope's light shimmer in the image of Seamus
Heaney's Rosie Keenan in his poem "At the Wellhead":

> Your songs, when you sing them with your two eyes
>   closed
> As you always do, are like a local road
> We've known every turn of in the past —
> That midge-veiled, high-hedged side-road where you
>   stood
> Looking and listening until a car
> Would come and go and leave you lonelier
> Than you had been to begin with. So, sing on,
> Dear shut-eyed one, dear far-voiced veteran,
>
> Sing yourself to where the singing comes from,
> Ardent and cut off like our blind neighbor
> Who played the piano all day in her bedroom.
> Her notes came out to us like hoisted water
> Ravelling off a bucket at the wellhead
> Where next thing we'd be listening, hushed and
>   awkward.
>
> That blind-from-birth, sweet-voiced, withdrawn
>   musician
> Was like a silver vein in heavy clay.
> Night water glittering in the light of day.
> But also just our neighbor, Rosie Keenan.
> She touched our cheeks. She let us touch her braille
> In books like books wallpaper patterns came in.

Her hands were active and her eyes were full
Of open darkness and a watery shine.

She knew us by our voices. She'd say she 'saw'
Whoever or whatever. Being with her
Was intimate and helpful like a cure
You didn't notice happening. When I read
A poem with Kennan's well in it, she said,
'I can see the sky at the bottom of it now.'[2]

---

2. Seamus Heaney, *The Spirit Level* (New York: Farrar Straus Giroux, 1996),
76–77.

T W O

May the God of hope bring you . . . joy and peace in your faith. . . . (Romans 15:13)

Walking Free

Ken lived in the woods in Oregon. He left Los Angeles because it got too crazy there. I think he was right. His parents supported him in his choice, though it could not have been easy for them. He was in the first group of university students I taught in Los Angeles over a dozen years ago. Because of his native intelligence he quickly mastered the principles of accounting that assured him a post with one of the major firms in southern California upon graduation. He did figures for a year. He had a bright and promising future and a girlfriend to make any mother proud. Indeed, his parents were proud of him and very happy.

But Ken was not happy in the figures business. Something deeper called to him. He thought once that it might be a call to the priesthood, but it was even deeper than that. He told me once that his vocation might be to seek, his whole life long, and, in the end, he committed himself to that search. That's what gave shape to his life.

He lived in the woods, teaching English to migrant

workers for a pittance, hiking on hidden trails in the Pacific Northwest without his clothes on. He had no clear idea of the road ahead of him, but he had given his life, his whole heart, to something. He was happy.

I learned about Ken's death through a stranger who tracked me down after finding my phone number in Ken's address book. He told me that Ken had been hiking alone on Mount Adams, and that he had fallen. This seemed strange because Ken was an experienced hiker. He had been missing for several days before forest rangers found his body down in a ravine. Ken's dog led friend Paul to his backpack and the journal in which he had written a few words just before he fell to his death.

I knew that he liked to hike. Earlier I had received letters every several weeks while he was on a six-month hike from the Baja peninsula in Mexico up the California coast to the Pacific Northwest. Later he wrote that he hiked every chance he got. He would rise early in the morning and climb to the highest point he could manage. And from there he would pray and write in his journal. It was while perched at prayer that he fell to his death on August 19, 1994.

Ken had adopted some of the spirituality of Native American peoples. And he came to be known as "Walking Free." I had assumed that the change in name was in part due to that influence, a bit like "Dances with Wolves." And to Bruce Cockburn, the Canadian rocker-prophet-poet whose lyrics inspired Ken back in those days in Los Angeles. Although I still have a slight suspicion that "Walking Free" had something to do with Ken's long hikes in his birthday suit, I understand now that most serious hikers take "trail names." Whatever the origin of the new name, that's how he came to be known and loved.

Hundreds of people attended memorial services in Oregon and later in southern California, where he is buried. A carpenter friend of Ken's made the casket. The pinewood is etched with mountains on front and back, with a bald eagle on one end and a hummingbird on the other. Feathers on each corner represent the four directions that Ken turned to when he prayed, and the inscription "Walking Free" lies across the top. The tombstone is etched with mountains, a waterfall, clouds, and trees and is marked with his Christian name and "Walking Free." The dates of his birth and death are inscribed, as is a small cross in the center. Thirty-two is much too young to die.

His parents expressed profound gratitude for the number of Ken's friends who had been so helpful to them. They were deeply touched by the memorial services in Oregon, and by the pledges of fidelity which, in fact, Ken's community of friends had begun to make good on. Times were rocky for Ken's parents. His mother's father had recently died and their other children's marriages were in trouble.

I can imagine nothing so painful as the loss of a child. The loss of a parent is earth-shattering, even when the death occurs in old age or after a long illness. We expect to bury our parents, even though we are never really prepared for it. But no mother or father ever expects to bury a child they brought into the world. "Words can't begin to express the terrible grief, the hurt, the ache, the insurmountable sadness we all experienced. Just how much could we handle? It was unbearable," Ken's mother said to me.

The other two children's marriages ended in divorce. It hurt Ken's parents to see their children twisted in pain and anger. Their relationships with their son-in-law and daughter-in-law had to be renegotiated. It's never quite the same after a divorce, and both couples had children.

Ken's mother writes from time to time and tells me that their world has fallen apart. They feel like everything has crumbled, that their world is in a shambles. She wants to turn back the clock. They have a lot of free time now, she says. They go for walks, alone. There aren't as many requests to baby-sit the grandchildren. They plan to return to Mount Adams year by year to mark the anniversary of Ken's dying. "We're going to climb that mountain as best we can. Ken's spirit is so alive in us, and I know we'll need his help."

Now retired, they live in beautiful southern California, free of the responsibilities and worries that plague newlyweds and young parents. But their golden years have been burdened with an unending ache known only to those who have lost a child, a pain compounded by the sight of their other two children's lives become a shambles. But they go on, as many others do. They are certain that they are guided by their son's spirit, walking with them every step of the way.

Going Through the Motions

She kept changing her name. Each time she joined a monastery, or left one, she wanted to be known by a different name. I couldn't keep track of them all and, at times, I didn't know what to call her because none of the names seemed to fit. All these different names made me cautious. They signaled instability. And she was unsettled, going from one monastery to another, from this institute to that, leaving one thing and then another. I was amazed that so many people were willing to give her another chance.

The first time we met she was in her early thirties and on her way into another monastery. She had been living on her own for several years, since she had been asked to leave a former community because she didn't really seem suited for the monastic life. Or it wasn't suited to her. "It's the celibacy thing," she said one time, smiling. There was more, of course, as I later came to know. But at the time we first met, she was ever so grateful that a newly elected abbess of a different monastery would receive her and let her try it out again. She felt anew her calling to a disciplined spiritual life.

When I came upon her several years later she had settled into the monastery, joined and stayed six or eight months. And then she had left, to face "issues," she said. After a short time, she asked if she could return. She was welcomed once more. This time, she assured me, she was "really settling in." She added that she wanted to keep her desire to wander in check, and that monastic stability was a good way to do this. What I liked most about her was the honesty. I began to understand why everyone was willing to give her another chance. She didn't posture; she simply told the truth about where she "was at." Who could refuse her?

But it didn't seem to last very long. Six months later, she narrated for me all that was inherently flawed in the Christian scheme of things: sin, suffering, the lack of true enlightenment among Christians, especially Christian monks and nuns. She had adopted a new kind of meditation practice, inspired by a branch of Buddhism whose name I could never master. She gave herself to it wholeheartedly, trying to reconcile her new practices with the heritage of Christian monasticism. On later visits, we would walk on the grounds of the monastery in the early evenings. Deer graced the lovely lawns. And she would talk to them sweetly, as if they were her children.

Something deep within me worried about her, and I sensed that she would be pulling up stakes once again. What could have been more congenial to a commitment to prayer and spiritual practice than this monastery? It seemed a perfect fit.

One day I said to her, "You know, if you leave, it's not fair to you or to anyone else to think about coming back here or to any other monastery." I didn't need to say much more. She did all the talking: "I don't believe in a personal God anymore. The whole Christian thing doesn't make any sense. And these nuns aren't enlightened. They only go through the motions; they are not being transformed. They don't engage in any real spiritual discipline. Monks and nuns who engage in genuine spiritual practice are really different. They become more peaceful, more tranquil, more centered."

I protested that participating in communal prayer seven times a day, beginning at 3:15 A.M., seemed a rather serious spiritual discipline to me. I said that I found it admirable that monks and nuns who didn't seem to be very "enlightened" still continued to pray throughout the day. I lauded them, even if some of them might indeed just "go through the motions." I let her know that I think that God may be glorified even when we just seem to go through the motions, doing what is ours to do, especially when there's not a whole lot of light coming our way. It's a way of enlightenment to just keep on going when there seems very little reward.

All my words were wasted. I knew it as I heard them leaving my mouth. She was convinced that she had found another way. The Christian world into which she was born and in which she was nurtured was now foreign territory. Its language of cross and resurrection had become a cacophony. Its symbols and values had begun to clutter up her mind. She wanted to be free from it. So she decided to leave again, in search of something else. And, yes, she changed her name again, naming herself by a Buddhist term that means "no name."

Before she left we entered the church for the closing prayer of the day. Bowing reverently before the altar, she took her place alongside all the other nuns in choir. I listened to the strength of her voice, lifted with the others in prayer to God. I wondered if Buddhists pray in the same way as Christians. What was wrong with going through the motions with these nuns who filled this church seven times a day, following in the footsteps of myriads of monastics throughout the ages?

"No Name" left her place in choir to light the candle before the statue of the Virgin Mary. She led the "Salve Regina," the closing hymn of the day. I could hear her voice clearly among the others and I found in its echo great consolation, knowing that sometimes we all must go through the motions, even as we look for a God to pray to.

Where Is God Today?

Early convictions about the order and sense of the world carried over into the modern period, even for those who did not believe in God. However, the conviction that the world makes sense and that we are headed toward a brighter future was identified with the human person rather than with God. People chose to rely on the powers of human reason rather than on God's providential care.

Nonetheless, the conviction that things make sense in view of a big picture remained strongly ingrained.

Is God Still in Charge?

Today, bold claims about the autonomous, rational human being and a view of history and the world that is coherent and intelligible, have been unsettled by the suffering experienced by individuals and by whole races and classes of people. Suffering interrupts our lives and disorients us profoundly. It causes us to question basic beliefs about order in the universe, divine providence, and the very nature of God. At times we cry out from the depth of suffering: Does the world make any sense? Is God really "in charge"?

More than anything else, it is the staggering horror of suffering, that of others and our own, that has shaken the foundations of our beliefs. The atrocities played out before our eyes on television unsettle the conviction that the world and human beings are essentially good, and that the power of love will ultimately prevail over evil. With atomic bombs dropped on cities, with genocide in Rwanda and Bosnia, we question whether history is really progressing. Our own experiences of loss and tragedy, the untimely deaths of those we love, or the onset of debilitating disease, and the sheer randomness of it all, stamp a bold question mark next to the very notion of God's providence.

If the premoderns and the moderns believed in a big picture, that things "hang together" and that God is in charge, from a postmodern perspective the world is in a shambles. Much of what made the world feel so secure and reliable has come undone. And the seepage affects just about everything and everyone in the human household.

It seems at times that we stand in the midst of ruins: in culture, society, politics, and even religion. The violence inflicted upon innocent millions, the massacre of entire races of people, the aggression of powerful races against the defenseless, the generations-old conflict in Northern Ireland, the horror of the AIDS epidemic, the banality of senseless crime, the obscenity of "gangsta" rap music, the blight of child prostitution and pornography — all these events baffle and disorient. For some, the shock of what actually goes on in their lives calls into question the existence of a good and loving God. As a people we are overwhelmed. We wonder whether anything we can do has real potential to make any difference whatsoever. We doubt whether we are able to make the world a better place for the next generation. And if a provident God is not "in charge," calling for a final reckoning, then why spend all the energies of heart, mind, and soul trying to make good on life? Why make good decisions? Why act responsibly? Why be loving? Why stay faithful until the end?

Finding reserves of hope is indeed a more complex task than in earlier generations. This is not because of some moral weakness on the part of people in today's world, but because those very things in which people once hoped seem so much less reliable now. Where is one's hope to be placed? The unreliable and the uncertain signal caution. Why stake my life's energies on something so shaky? Is it reasonable to still hold on in hope?

Today, as the twentieth century draws to an end, young people are often berated for their indifference. It has ever been thus. But in our day hopelessness among the young seems to bear the marks of a chronic illness. Many would say that it all started in the 1960s. As a "relic of the 1960s," my generation is often said to be at the root of the problem. In this view the seeds of the problem were sown back in the '60s when some persons challenged the legitimacy of an undeclared war, thereby stirring questions about loyalty to their own country. The "sexual liberation" caused many persons to disregard long-venerated traditions of sexual conduct and mores. Those involved in the Civil Rights movement clashed with normative patterns of social arrangements among different racial groups. Women's liberation posed a fundamental assault on common perceptions and tightly held convictions about male-female relations. And in the aftermath of Vatican II, religious women in the Roman Catholic church went from billowy black dresses and foot-length veils to smart suits and closely cropped hair, sometimes in a matter of months. In each of these instances, it seemed to some that too much was lost and so little was gained. Some became disillusioned. Others gave up, feeling betrayed and wounded by their church or by God.

Is There a Way Out?

The problem many of us face is our inability to move with any clear conviction into the future. In large part the postmodern consciousness is a reaction, finding its bearings and drawing its energy from the values of the modernity it rejects. What postmodernity proposes as a solution is quite difficult to pin down. In fact, it is near impossible to name any one course for the future. The postmodern mind knows that there is something fundamentally wrong with modern ways of perceiving and being, but what alternatives are there?

Some are inclined to say that it is no longer possible to trust our institutions and structures to carry commonly held meanings, purposes, and values. In place of these there is instead a variety of prisms through which different individuals look at reality. These prisms are themselves molded by the self-interests of those in positions of power. The task is to expose the power mongers and "deconstruct" or dismantle their views of the world that keep the poor voiceless and invisible and the powerless weak. The "deconstructionist" mandate is to bring to light the inability of all structures, institutions, and language to convey authentic meaning, purpose, value. In such a view the task is to recognize that the whole house is in a shambles, to tear it down and clear it away so that something utterly new can stand in its place. In most deconstructionist approaches there are few, if any, "givens." There seem to be no foundations, no basic referents such as the self, or God, or a correspondence between truth claims and truth itself, which merit our trust and in which our hope can be placed.

Thus the mood today. Feeling that things are breaking apart more than hanging together, sensing limits rather than possibilities, aware of the contingency of human existence more than its stability, preoccupied more with change than with the permanent, the postmodern person is cautious. The most that can be expected is a passing encounter with someone or something in which to hope — for now. Then the uneasiness will return, along with the need to pack up and move on once again. As impermanence, fragmentation, disruption, interruption, disorientation, randomness, and uncertainty fill the air, confidence loses ground. Even the possibility of some new order that will hold the center together is no longer anticipated. And hope dims.

But there is another approach to what we call modernity. Some persons recognize that it is possible to articulate or to construct meaningful and purposeful, coherent and reliable worldviews. But unlike previous frameworks these new ones will not have quite the same persuasiveness or universal applicability. Nor will they last as long. Structures and institutions that convey meaning will be helpful in different places and times but will not be able to appeal to human experience in any universal way, nor for very long. In other words, our claims to truth and meaning and value will be more partial, modest, even humble.

Even though many of the deconstructionist approaches in the postmodern period are nihilistic — more interested in tearing down than in building up — nonetheless, they have important consequences for our understanding of hope. Since Christian life is concerned with cultivating the deepest reserves of human hope grounded in faith in the resurrection of Jesus Christ, even and especially when everything is lost and when there seems to be no apparent reason to be hopeful, both "constructionist" and "deconstructionist" currents can offer Christians insights in their efforts to articulate a reason for hope even in the shambles of our time.

How Is God Present Today?

Like the force of the ocean's undertow, there are fundamental religious issues at the bottom of these currents. While some people are not aware of the postmodern mood and others recognize features of it mixed together with elements of the premodern and modern, there are many more who sense its powerful grip on their lives. A growing number of people have increasing difficulty conceiving of a God who stands untouched above the sufferings of millions. They search for signs of God's benevolent presence in their own lives and in the lives of their loved ones, lives that keep breaking down in so many different, unexpected, unanticipated ways. They try to discern God's will expressed in structures, institutions and authorities. But these are splintering apart at the core. They are stunned by the boldness of others who claim that God's preordained plan is steadily unfolding throughout history and that justice and goodness and beauty are actually on the increase — all appearances to the contrary.

The interruptive character of history, the capacity of suffering to disorient and baffle, the discontinuities between expectation and event, all seem to boldly question the grounds of Christian hope. But the recognition that traditional human conceptions of order and providence are no longer plausible, and that promises made by rational self-sufficient individuals have failed to satisfy the deepest longings of the human heart, does not inevitably entail abandoning hope. It *does* entail recognizing a self that is more fragile *and* a God who is both strong and vulnerable. In other words, acknowledging the loss of what has been familiar can be the very foundation for the possibility of constructing or articulating new understandings of God, human life, history, the world, and the relation between God and the world.

Today, where is the God of modernity, the God who is "in charge" of the universe, the God who can be counted on to intervene and help us out? This God is the Supreme Being who rules the world. With sphinx-like inscrutability, God exerts power as an absolute monarch. Power here is understood as the ability to do whatever one chooses, forcibly if necessary. Divine power is not to be questioned because, unlike other expressions of power, God's power is always exercised to achieve noble, even if incomprehensible, purposes. God is "in control," intervening in human life and history in order to bring about worthy ends.

At the crossroads of modernity and postmodernity, this understanding of God is simply beyond belief. Consequently, increasing numbers of people face a profound sense of loss of this familiar understanding of God. They wonder about where and how God is present, and this haunts them. Along with this comes a deep uncertainty about one's place in the world, a place once assured in the tightly knit views and social arrangements of premodernity and modernity. In the ache of this loss, the sense of absence and disorientation brought on when one cleans house of implausible understandings of God, the question emerges as if for the first time: How can I speak the name of God in prayer? How can I call out to God in the midst of such unbearable suffering?

Raising these questions does not imply that there is no God. But these questions, brought on by the crumbling of our belief in the God of modernity, must be raised. It is in the midst of such a collapse, in the ruins of an understanding of God which is more idolatrous than theonomous, that we can "lean into" a new experience of God known in the ache of absence. Here, at this juncture of knowing and unknowing, of light and dark, a dazzling darkness summons us to what may be known of God at the limits of what we have known until now.

The darkness is a moment of disclosure. The experience of absence is a kind of presence. In the early moments of prayer we might be inclined to search for signs of the unfolding preordained universal plan of salvation being enacted throughout a history in which "God writes straight with crooked lines." But in the deeper movements of prayer we can only squint to catch a glimpse of God's unfathomable mystery discerned in episodic and sporadic acts of compassion, justice, and hope in a world-become-a-shambles.

What is called for at this point is the cultivation of deep reserves of hope in a hidden God rather than a return to the securities of the premodern and modern ages. Or, worse, an appeal to an understanding of God which, for the most part, cannot be believed. None of it rings true any longer.

Is There Room Enough for Hope?

It is precisely in these experiences of vulnerability and loss that the stirrings of hope are often first recognized. When everything is lost, when there seems to be no way out and no reason whatsoever to go on, it is especially then that hope has a chance. The deepest kind of hope begins when we are really at the end, when our face is slammed up against the wall, when our sense of self is shaken, when the world seems unreliable, when our relationships are strained or shattered, when God seems no longer to be in the heavens and absolutely nothing seems right with the world. Sometimes it is then and only then that hope, this mysterious capacity in us to open up to some other future possibility, begins. Not always, but sometimes. And perhaps that is reason enough for us to take the next step, to peek around the corner, to turn to the next page, to pray.

T H R E E

These sufferings bring patience, as we know, and patience brings perseverance, and perseverance brings hope, and this hope is not deceptive, because the love of God has been poured into our hearts by the Holy Spirit which has been given us. (Romans 5:4–5)

The Talk in Tinsel Town

My sister said Ellen bleached her hair, but I didn't think so. I thought it was very possible for a Scandinavian in her mid-thirties to still have platinum blonde hair. And ten years later, in her mid-forties, Ellen's hair is still shimmering blonde. But my sister didn't like her to begin with. Mother didn't like her either, and said she was overbearing. Nearly everyone said the same thing. In fact, she could be shrill in stating her opinions. People were turned off. A friend once said that hearing her state her theological views was like listening to a hysterical person placing an emergency call to 911. But I liked her.

She was bright. My God, was she bright! She had just finished her doctorate at the University of Chicago and began teaching where I did. We were both about thirty and joined the faculty at the same time. Years later we would laugh and say that we grew up together in Los Angeles. After all, life supposedly begins at thirty. And as they say in LA, "There is no life east of Sepulveda Boulevard"; Los Angeles is the beginning, the middle, and the end. Ellen

loved Los Angeles, "because it's so tacky." I was more am-
bivalent. I loved the weather and the lure of the ocean,
but I found the whole place wacky. We drove around with
the top down, even in February and March, visiting the
beach, and we talked without end.

We shared the growing pains of learning how to teach
theology, a subject in which very few students had any
discernible interest. Then there were the more painful
lessons to be learned in dealing with colleagues and students. And there were also the more important of life's
lessons to learn about: deep desires; struggling with ill
health; falling and failing in love; naming and owning the
truth of who we were. Many of these lessons we learned
together.

A child of immigrants, she had been badly scarred by
something that had gone wrong in the early days of her
life. She had been jilted in love more times than she dared
tell. In addition to her deep psychic wounds, she had been
sick for long stretches of time. Sometimes I thought that
she was so bright because she had had nothing else to
do but read and think during long illnesses that kept her
bedridden as a child and then a teenager. From the beginning, I knew somehow that beneath the shrill and steely
surface Ellen was utterly vulnerable.

In those first years of our teaching I excelled while
she seemed to stumble at every step. She simply couldn't
understand students who didn't want to learn, students
who instead wanted good jobs, fine houses on the beach,
and new, shiny cars. How can you teach someone who

is not interested in learning? She couldn't comprehend it. Then there was the price she paid for speaking her mind. If she knew that telling it straight always had a price tag, it didn't really matter. She simply told the truth. It never dawned on her to do otherwise.

Only rarely did we talk about theology, though on the face of it this should have been our strongest common interest. There were too many other things to talk about: the David Hockney exhibit at the Los Angeles County Museum of Art, the film *Babette's Feast,* Kiri Te Kanawa's mixed parentage and her voice, the likes of which I had never heard before.

I knew that her perspective on religion was quite different from mine. She had studied religion in a large secular university, and I had studied sacred theology at the Catholic University of America. We listened carefully to one another's thoughts, lectures, and articles-in-preparation, but we never really engaged each other's ideas or challenged each other's assumptions. In many ways, we really didn't know where each other stood on the most basic questions theologians wrestle with. I felt, though, that I had a hunch about "where she was at."

Even LA's bright shiny days could not save Ellen from slumping into serious depressions. Things were still not going well; despite her best efforts, the semester had yielded another batch of negative teaching evaluations, and her two-year romance was doomed to failure, even though neither of them had the strength or courage to walk away.

But this was LA. The sun was shining, even in February, and the words of the surprise Grammy-winner were pumping through every stereo on Hollywood Boulevard: "Don't worry, be happy!" We went for a long drive under a bright blue sky. Stuck in traffic, as is almost always the case in LA, we were shaded from the sun's blaze by walls of skyscrapers on both sides of Wilshire Boulevard. I listened to her. I looked at the brilliant sky that was squandered on her. She didn't even know it was there.

I took a shallow breath and said a few words about suffering as I put on yet another layer of sunscreen, and then added a few faltering words about the gospel being all about hope. About how growth and transformation take place in and through our suffering, not around it, but *in* and *through* it. This is the central mystery of Christian faith, I added. The cross is God's promise that suffering and death are not the final word. I tried to say all this with composure and dispassion, even though I believed it with my whole heart and soul and still do.

Ellen came clean: "I'm not a Christian anymore. I can't believe in God. Can't you see that the cross just glorifies suffering? People need to get out of suffering. What's so good about suffering? Why do happiness and fulfillment have to come *in* and *through* suffering? Suffering should be avoided, not embraced."

I had even less to say. "But God is with us in our suffering," I feebly pointed out. Her voice suddenly grew shrill. It screeched out the deep pain that her critics had never sensed: "If God is in suffering, then he's not God. The point is that God is supposed to help us out of our suffering. Why would God be in suffering? If he can't stop suffering, then he's not God. And if he doesn't stop it, why believe in God? Why believe in God if he doesn't *do* something to help you? I don't believe in God because God does nothing to help me. Nothing."

We've remained friends over the years and across the miles. She's not miserable any longer. Things can change. She found her heart's desire in the love of a man to whom she is now happily married. She still teaches religious studies, but she is less shrill, though she still has no faith in God. Whenever we are together we don't talk about what occupied us that day tooling around Tinsel Town. Our friendship was and is rooted in something much deeper than our differing religious convictions.

We matured together and, like so many others, we both left Los Angeles for other destinations, literally and figuratively, although I have since returned. We both grew in the strength of our different convictions. Ellen's abandonment of the Christian faith has matured; it is now full and complete. And I have continued to hold fast to the Word nailed to a cross, even when God seems to do nothing for me, when God doesn't seem to help me or answer my plea. I believe simply because God is God.

We have found hope in quite different places. She has found hope in life and life alone. My hope is in a promise that there is more than meets the eye, that things are often other than what they seem to be. Though we live in different worlds, hope is the language by which we braid a bridge between them. Hope is part of a language that she had lost in those days in Tinsel Town, but has now learned to speak once again.

What Is Hope?

It is too simplistic to suggest that people today have no hope or that the young, and the not-so-young, are unable to make and keep commitments. People cannot live without hope, and they will not flourish without being committed to something or someone. People can live without faith and apparently many do. Many also live without love. But without hope, something to move us forward, we simply cannot go on. Hope is a way of making good on life. By hoping, we give shape to our lives, even when our specific hopes for this or that are shattered, when our dreams are destroyed or our lives seem to be coming undone. Hope still remains.

At this moment in history, making good on life is no easy or straightforward matter. Many of us feel uncertain about the reliability of our cherished institutions — family, church, community, home town — to carry, nurture, and sustain our deepest desires. Oftentimes we feel that we are left without a compass in the middle of a journey. The directions used to be obvious and the path was clearly marked. Even the guides, in whom our forebears placed their full confidence, seem unreliable. At times our trust has been blatantly betrayed as cherished persons and communities have been tainted with scandals heretofore unimagined. This makes it seem as if the beacons of light along the way have been snuffed out. The journey becomes much more difficult when the signposts are barely recognizable, and many landmarks are irreparably tarnished.

Indeed, the metaphor of life as a journey, which implies that there is a place of destination, something to look forward to, some point at the end, seems up for grabs. Is "journey" any longer a fitting description of the Christian way? Where will I be when I get to where I'm headed? People are raising such questions as never before. They are unsure and quite cautious of those who offer clear-cut, definitive answers to such complex questions. In the end, we know it isn't going to be that easy.

What is this "thing" without which we cannot live, without which we have no reason to go on? A story told me by my grandmother may capture something of the meaning of hope. As a very poor farm girl growing up in the hinterlands of Ireland's northwesternmost coast, it was quite common for her and the others in the family to go to bed hungry after having worked in the fields from dawn till dusk. Meat was usually in short supply, and potatoes, the staple of the Irish diet, were not always abundant. Milk was often scarce, and butter was sheer luxury.

Year by year, as the days became colder and darker in the drawing near of winter, her father would set a candle in the window in anticipation of Christmas. In the aftermath of one very bad harvest, when nearly everything that had been planted had not yielded fruit, there was hardly anything in the cupboards. But on Christmas Eve, amidst the protests of his family, my great-grandfather took a bit of butter, melted it on a little plate, lit the wick of his makeshift candle, and placed it in the window. The family was shocked. His response to them was quite simple: "We know that we can get by on a little food for several weeks. We've done it before. A little water and milk can keep us going for several days. That we also know. But, listen to me now and listen to me good, we cannot go on for one day without hope."

Hope in Scripture and Theology: The Middle Child

Hope is the very heart and center of a human being. There is simply nothing more central to human life. But, strangely, we human beings who need hope more than anything else in life have written so little about it. In a good deal of Christian theology, hope seems to be something like a proverbial "middle child," sandwiched in between affirmations about the priority of faith and the excellence of love. Since hope was the original impulse of theology, the relatively meager attention given to hope is particularly striking. It was precisely in anticipating, waiting, hoping for the return of Christ in glory that members of the early Christian communities began to reflect on the meaning and message of Jesus.

In the New Testament, hope emerges at the intersection of what has been accomplished in Christ and what is still to be, what may be called the "already" and the "not yet." Early Christian life was all about waiting in the confidence of faith in Christ. In the words of the Epistle to the Hebrews: "Now faith is the assurance of things hoped for, the conviction of things not seen" (Hebrews 11:1). As time passed, though, Christ's coming in glory became a more remote, albeit very real, expectation. And in time, living "in Christ" took the place of expecting the coming of Christ in the near future.

In the early Christian communities, as Christ's coming in glory seemed to be delayed indefinitely, their understanding of hope changed. Christians began to realize that their hope had to include patient waiting. Hope came to be understood more as an immense openness toward the promised future, a future affirmed by faith and realized through God's saving acts in history in and through the person of Jesus Christ. History — what actually goes on in the world — came to be seen as the place where hope is enacted.

As the church and Christian tradition were shaped through the centuries, it was Saint Augustine who, perhaps inadvertently, eclipsed the early expectation of the "end time," the second coming of Christ, by his empha-

sis on Christian life within the church. At the risk of
making a gross simplification, it might be said that for
Saint Augustine the church was the Kingdom of God on
earth. In subsequent Christian history, hope became more
and more identified with the church, especially with its
teaching office, scripture, the bishop, and the priest. Hope
became confined to the visible church. Though there have
been some notable exceptions, hope has not played an
explicit, central role in the writings of either Christian
theologians or historians.

Many Christians appeal to the writings of the apostle
Paul in asserting that while in the end three things last —
faith, hope, and love — the "greatest of these is love"
(1 Corinthians 13:13). Properly understood, faith, hope,
and love are of a piece. The distinctions we make among
the three theological virtues only serve to help us understand different dimensions of a single reality, the reality
of the human person's relationship to God. This relationship is possible because of God's gift to us of faith, hope,
and love, and our response to this gift.

Indeed, there is a great deal of overlap among them.
On the one hand, there is considerable similarity between hope, confidence, and trust, although confidence
and trust are most often associated with faith. On the
other hand, hope is quite close to desire, waiting, and
longing, which are most often associated with love. So,
is there anything truly distinctive about hope? Is there
something about the human person and the relationship between the human person and God that is properly

named "hope" in contrast to what we name "faith" and
"love"?

The Distinct Character of Hope

Hope is the very condition for the possibility of believ-
ing and loving. It is openness to the light of faith and
to the action of love. Hope is the capacity in each of us
that is open to God's truth and love. It is that quality in
the human being that is open to possibility, to new things
happening.

Hope is also the driving force of all human initiative,
the undercurrent of all human activity. It impels and pro-
pels. It looks for the coming of the new, that which has
never been before. Hope is the dynamism that carries us
from now to then, inclining us to look from the present
to the future, from what is to what is still to come, and
on to what might yet be. Hope is the great virtue of the
human person *in via*, on the way. The betrayal of hope
lies in despair as anticipated failure and in presumption
as anticipated fulfillment. In both betrayals of hope, tra-
ditionally known as sins against hope, we try to deny our
existence as pilgrims, wanting instead to assure the end
results, control what lies beyond us, and have our lives
otherwise than from the hand of God.

In trying to understand hope, one of the difficulties we
face is the fact that the English language has only one
word to describe a complex and rich reality. "Hope" is a
term pregnant with meanings. We might hope it doesn't

rain or snow. We might hope to do well in an interview. We might say to the bank teller, "Hope you have a nice day!" We can also hope that our health holds or that our children are preserved from illness or an accident, or that a friend's surgery is successful. Here, we draw closer to the deeper meanings of hope — hope as a movement within the human person that sees the present and all its prospects, or lack thereof, in the light of some other prospect, something good, or even slightly better, that is to come. It recognizes that what is presently possible might not be all that there is. Hope holds out and holds on. It looks in expectation toward some other — a person, a thing, an event, a time, or a state — in the realization that, if and when it does come, it comes only as a gift.

This kind of hope is rooted in the conviction that there is still more to be said and that there might yet be some good news. Hope waits and it longs for more. It looks to the next moment, and the next. Hope always moves through and beyond the present moment. It is not restlessness, but anticipation.

Too often we are inclined to think of hope as an emergency virtue. When things are really bad or when we have nothing else, there is always hope. Hope is something that we tend to save up for a crisis. Indeed, it is true that hope is what we have, precisely when we do not have something else. And hope may spring forth at the very moment when we are really at the end of our rope. It is precisely in those times when we are really "on the edge," when we are most prone to despair, that we can lean into hope and rise, moving past darkness and despair in and through hoping. But it is also true that hope is present in each moment of daily, mundane, ordinary life as we look to the next.

Hope, in this deep and strong sense, is not the same as the lightheartedness we feel when things are going well for ourselves or for our loved ones. Nor is this deep hope at the root of our willingness to invest energy in tasks that apparently have a good chance to succeed. Hope, rather, is the capacity to work for something, to continually "go for it," simply because it is good, desirable, or "worthy" — and *not* because we have a fairly good chance of succeeding, and not necessarily because there may be some juicy reward in it for us. The more desperate the situation in which we demonstrate hope, the more forbidding the circumstances, the greater the odds against things turning out well, the deeper the hope. The more hopeless the present may appear to be, the more ardent our hope for something better.

Hope is most assuredly not the same as happy-go-lucky optimism. And it is not a forced chumminess or a saccharine naïveté in the face of incontrovertible facts. Hope is not the dogged defiance that everything will turn out well — "By damn, I will make it so!" Rather, hope is the serene conviction that something makes sense, that it's worth it, regardless of how it might turn out.

Practicing Hope

Even though hope lies at the core of every human life, it is first and finally a gift, like life itself. Though hope is a gift, it demands that we recognize it as such, accept it, cooperate with it, make it our own. Hope is a virtue, a theological virtue explicitly and directly concerned with our relationship to God. It is at once a gift and our activity. We grow in hope precisely by being hopeful, by acting hopefully. Hope must be exercised, even in the face of what seems to be hopeless, and especially in the face of our own feelings of hopelessness. Now, how do we grow in hope?

There are three elements in the act of hope. Or, said another way, hope moves through three steps. The first is the recognition that what I hope for I do not yet possess or see with any clarity. Second, I recognize that what I hope for may be difficult to achieve. Third, I see that even though what I hope for may be difficult, seemingly beyond my grasp, I do stand some chance of having it. It just might be possible. Hope is always directed to a future good that is hard but not absolutely impossible to attain.

Hope strains ahead, rooted in the conviction that there may be a way out of whatever difficulty is at hand, that things can work out even though it may appear to the contrary. Hope is that inextricable sense of the possible, of what might be. Without guarantees, hope struggles to find a way over each hurdle, one by one, and to find or make a path past every dead end. Hope emerges as our own resources seem to fail us, when we come undone in the presence of a paralyzing situation that seems without possibility. What brings us to despair is the feeling that we are at an impasse from which there is no escape. Yet, even if we are stopped in our tracks, hope finds a way.

Hope, Faith, and Love

In an explicitly Christian sense, hope rests on what has already been affirmed by faith. Faith makes the first move. I say, "Yes, I do believe," and put my hope in what I have affirmed. But what happens when what I have affirmed in faith is no longer believable? What happens to hope when faith is shattered, when one's beliefs crumble? Without faith, how can hope be anchored? If the all-loving, all-knowing, all-powerful God is beyond belief in light of the enormity of human suffering and pain, is hope in God to be jettisoned along with the tattered and shattered belief in such a God?

It is precisely in the weakness of faith, even in the loss of faith, that we uncover the deepest meaning of hope. The deepest kind of hope goes on hoping precisely when there is no consolation to be drawn from it. Real hope does not constantly look for assurances of God's nearness, nor does hope try to determine how God's providential plan is being manifested in one's life, in the lives of others, or in the world at large. Hope may even take the form of challenging traditional explanations of God's will. By hope we navigate through the mistake of taking the hiddenness and silence of God for the nonexistence of God. Hope remains open to all new and often astonishing manifestations of the divine life, even the presence of God that may be known in the experience of absence or utter darkness.

Karl Rahner, arguably the most significant Roman Catholic theologian of the twentieth century, has written on the nature of hope. Rahner's insight, put in very simple terms, is that our *faith* in God is expressed in the affirmation of certain truths about God, and our *love* of God is expressed in and through our love of neighbor. But the nature of *hope* is different, says Rahner. Hope is more immediate, more direct in the human person's relationship with God. It is more basic, more fundamental. Hope does not hope in God or for God, but "Hope hopes God." Nothing more, nothing less.

Taking a cue from Rahner, we can conclude that hope remains even when the "what" or "whom" of our belief is no longer believed, or even when we no longer love the object or recipient of our love. But hope does remain. And it hopes no less than God—beyond belief and beyond our loving God or neighbor.

Each of us must remember that hope goes on when there seems to be nothing else. It is often a mere shaft of light in profound darkness or a sliver of a smile amidst an all-consuming gloom. Gerard Manley Hopkins, a poet who knew the depths of despair, kept on writing in the darkness even after the candle had gone out. Though the hope seemed to have gone out of him, especially during

his years in Dublin's "joyless city," his poetic voice lives
and beckons us to hope.

Nondum

God, though to Thee our psalm we raise
No answering voice comes from the skies;
To Thee the trembling sinner prays
But no forgiving voice replies;
Our prayer seems lost in desert ways.
Our hymn in the vast silence dies. . . .

And Thou art silent, whilst Thy world
Contends about its many creeds. . . .

My hand upon my lips I lay;
The breast's desponding sob I quell;
I move along life's tomb-decked way
And listen to the passing bell.
Summoning men from speechless day
To death's more silent, darker spell.

Oh till Thou givest that sense beyond,
To show Thee that Thou art, and near,
Let patience with her chastening wand
Dispel the doubt and dry the tear;
And lead me child-like by the hand
If still in darkness not in fear.

Speak! whisper to my watching heart
One word — as when a mother speaks

> Soft, when she sees her infant start,
> Till dimpled joy steals o'er its cheeks.
> Then, to behold Thee as Thou art,
> I'll wait till morn eternal breaks.[3]

Although there are some extended theological treatments of hope, it seems some of the most compelling images of hope are found in poetry, such as Charles Péguy's *The Portal to the Mystery of Hope.* One portion of this long poem, a monologue of God, states that God is best glorified in hope, for it is in hoping that a person expresses most profoundly the greatest trust in God, the greatest confidence in God's love for us.

> The faith that I love the best, says God, is hope.
>
> Faith doesn't surprise me.
> It's not surprising. . . .
> Charity, says God, that doesn't surprise me.
> It's not surprising. . . .
> But hope, says God, that is something that surprises
>   me.
> Even me.
> That is surprising.[4]

Hope, that which is deepest in us, may seem all the more surprising in a world that seems to be coming apart at the seams, a world which appears to offer little reason

---

3. From *Hopkins: Poems and Prose* (New York: Alfred Knopf, 1995), 47–49.
4. Grand Rapids: Eerdmans, 1996, 5–7.

for the hope. How do we begin to hope? What is necessary if we are to hope again after hope has been lost, after what is deepest in us has died? Hope begins where hope begins. And begin it does, again, and again and again.

FOUR

Work for the Lord with untiring effort and with great earnestness of spirit. If you have hope, this will make you cheerful. Do not give up if trials come; and keep on praying.

(Romans 12:11–12)

And They Lived

We were boyhood friends. On the face of it, I guess I
took religion a little more seriously than Kevin. He would
go to church every now and then, but he was more inclined to nature walks and sunsets as times for meeting
God or the sacred or the spirit. Kevin was never quite
sure what to call it. We chose different paths. He married
early. Joy's whole being was true to her name. I was in
the wedding party. I've been a groomsman nearly a dozen
times, and each time I'd weep a little bit, rejoicing as a
friend made a strong and binding commitment. I've always taken the business of being "best man" seriously. All
of these friends hear from me on their anniversaries. I've
stood and watched as their babies were christened, and
sometimes when their babies had babies. And now and
then, I've watched a commitment made with great and
boundless confidence crumble.

Kevin and Joy lived in a little apartment not far from
where we grew up. I was in college at the time, and Kevin
was already working a tough job. My head was filled with

fresh and, what I considered to be, brilliant ideas that I would talk to him about at length. In the beginning he seemed interested, but as his hands grew redder and redder, his palms more and more calloused and cut up from his work on highway construction, his mind seemed to wander as I went on and on. Sometimes it seemed as if he deliberately tuned me out. Once as he listened to my philosophical ramblings, he blurted out: "I only believe in Joy. My Joy. Whatever faith I have is in her."

Long years of silence followed. We hadn't had a falling out. It was simply the kind of silence of passing years that have taken you in different directions. Time seems to make us different people, and we wonder if we still have anything in common with our best friends of long ago. I had signed Kevin's high school yearbook "Smooth Sailing on the Ship of Success." And Kevin had signed mine with equally touching wishes: "Always remember the good times we had [then follows the list of all the shenanigans we both pulled during high school]! Always stay in touch. Your best bud, Kevin."

I was home for the holidays and a little nostalgic. I regretted not having seen Kevin for over ten years. I tracked down his phone number through his parents. Their generation didn't seem to move around as much as ours did.

His house was cold. "I don't spend much time here anymore. I work most of the time and go to the mountains on the weekends when I can. Still like that sort of thing." He offered tea or coffee. He put the water on to boil and rinsed out two mugs from the sink full of dishes. I couldn't help but notice the emptiness of Kevin's house. Even the kitchen seemed empty, joyless.

"She left me you know. She said she just didn't want to be married anymore." I remember seeing their wedding photo and wondered where that photo was now. Joy had been a lovely bride.

The dozen years since I had seen or spoken with my "best bud" melted away. I drew him near, gave him a big bear hug and gently kissed the side of his neck like my father used to do to me. "Tell me about it."

As the tea warmed us, the years continued to melt. "She came home one day and said she'd changed her mind." That was the beginning. Kevin wondered aloud if there had been earlier signs. He thought that they had agreed that marriage was until death. How could she just change her mind? But, as Kevin continued to talk, there was more to learn. Joy had fallen in love with a woman. She said she had avoided coming to terms with it and thought marrying Kevin would make things different. She thought it would change her feelings. But it didn't.

"She just didn't want to be married anymore. Couldn't see the point of sticking it out. I told her I understood, even that part, and that I would stay with her. I would always love her, no matter what." Kevin showed no trace of tears. I wondered if his heart had grown as tough and calloused as his hands, or if his tears had simply been all used up.

Kevin and Joy had been the proverbial couple on top of

the wedding cake. A perfect match, a handsome couple. If ever you could bet your money on a "and they lived happily ever after" couple, this was the one. But something had gone amuck. Their life together had come undone.

"When did things start to go wrong?" was my only question. Kevin said, without hesitation, "We began to lose respect for each other. You can love someone, but it's all twisted if you don't respect them."

She had chosen to follow another path, to try to make good on life in a way that has a different name than marriage. "She's had lots of regrets," he said. "She came back and said she wanted to start over, that the other pull wasn't as strong as she thought. Said we had had something good and that she wanted to get it back." But it was too late for Kevin. Something had gone out of him, died. He had nothing left for Joy. They couldn't get back together, even if it meant living alone with a sink full of dirty dishes from Monday through Friday.

He was down in the dumps most of the time. He came home from work, had pizza delivered some nights, drank lots of beer, and went to sleep. Then he got up the next day and did it again, and again. Sometimes he went to church.

He seemed so dragged out that I wondered if he was near total despair. So I wrote and called regularly. I didn't want to let another dozen years pass by. Some years later I invited him to come and visit me.

In the intervening years he had found the hidden reserves of a new joy. Something in him got stirred up by another woman to whom he could give his whole heart and soul. Once more he had something to live for. I heard all about her as we rode the roller coaster at Space Mountain at Disneyland, so far away from the street corners of Northeast Philadelphia where we had grown up. Kevin had met her one day after church. She had a little girl and was divorced. They had hopes of getting married but had agreed to take it one day at a time. If it worked out, they would each apply for an annulment. "It's important to both of us," Kevin said, "but if I don't get an annulment, I'm still gonna marry her anyway." And he did.

Together they live in the country of marriage, a terrain that is not recognized by their church. And so they make their own way in the church. To maintain his commitment to his beloved, Kevin lives at the edges of the church of his childhood, a church that came to mean so much to him when he was really down. "It helped me a lot. I believed what they said about God's forgiveness. Completely. But my deepest faith is in Regina's love. I believe in Gina."

Regina gave birth to Kevin's first child, Anthony. They go to church sometimes and bring the baby with them. "I still like to go. So does Regina. We don't go to communion, but we want Tony to be baptized. We don't think he should be out of the loop because of Gina and me. It feels like they're punishing him because of us. We named him for the church up the corner, you know. That's where I met Gina. You need God. Especially in the hard times."

Kevin is making good on life through his commitment

to Regina, at the margins of the church. He is more committed to the church than ever before, and to his beloved. Kevin has risen from rubble, a beacon to countless others whose lives are shattered by love's dying.

The Rebirth of Hope: Making Room for the Other

In this age of profound disillusionment, what are the conditions for the recovery of hope? In our lives as persons and as a people, what is necessary for hope to come alive again? How is hope retrieved once it has been lost or betrayed?

Much of what we used to count on for our sense of identity and belonging no longer helps. Structures, institutions, organizations are breaking down; in some cases they have already broken down. In the face of this breakdown — of what once was but is no more — there is a natural tendency to panic. In a way it's like moving from a familiar neighborhood or quitting a job. Nearly always we lament the absence of what was once so sure and reliable. The tendency toward cynicism or despair becomes more pronounced. Some persons come completely undone by such change.

Perhaps one way to understand what is happening in

our age is to think about forms — thought forms, family structures, religious institutions, educational systems — emptying themselves. We may see them breaking down and coming apart, which is generally judged to be very bad news. But as these institutions and structures become void of meaning or purpose or value, perhaps there is something to be gained from this very emptying. Perhaps it is that so much of what we have counted on, what we have relied upon and trusted, is breaking down and becoming empty because it cannot hold God. God cannot be grasped and dissected, let alone managed and controlled, by our thought forms, structures, or institutions. God is always and everywhere overspilling them all. God is too big, even for our organizational strategies or our five-year plans!

When we look at it this way, the emptying of structures and institutions characteristic of our age can be the occasion for a resurgence of hope. If we are to hope and move toward the future, we must recognize that God is not behind us, but always ahead of us, leaving traces and clues of the divine presence. But even as we look for traces of God's nearness, the presence of God can never be tied down or identified with any structure, organization, or thought form, even the church. As the forms splinter around us, the person with the deepest kind of hope takes confidence in realizing that God is more than any form or structure. God's presence overspills. This, then, is a reason for hope. So we must look beyond the forms. We must learn new ways of perceiving and being in the world, and it is the emptiness, at times, that can help us discern God's presence. There it lies, in those moments, persons, events, and efforts where we least expect it. And there and then the reason for our hope is found.

Conditions for the Recovery of Hope

An admission of failure, that we cannot do it all by ourselves, will start us on the way to finding a rebirth of hope. We must admit that our culture of individualism, our unrelenting restlessness, and our bottom-line pragmatism have failed to satisfy the deepest longings of our hearts. Unbridled individualism does not work and has disastrous consequences. Perhaps we've been sold a bad bill of goods and are still paying the cost. Rather than educating the whole person to live a good, virtuous life, our schools have become places for skills-training and for developing techniques to more effectively render "services" from "provider" to "consumer." The medical profession has become the health care industry. Our religious institutions are often far removed from their raison d'être: some have become spiritual support groups; others have become social service ministries. It is not that this in itself is bad; it's just that religious institutions must be more than this. The rebirth of hope requires that we admit the truth that the way we have done it up till now and the way we continue to do things simply does not work.

Admitting breakdown and failure in the culture at large is not unlike what sometimes happens in our own lives.

In the earlier stages of life, we work to give shape to a sense of self. Our personal identity is often hard won, and not easily given up. We work very hard to become who we are: a dutiful daughter, a loyal son, a fine teacher, a trustworthy friend, a person of integrity, a man of good reputation, a woman as good as her word, a person of some distinction. And if in the middle of the life that we have worked so hard to achieve, the self we built and have become falls apart, we are shattered. Some call it a nervous breakdown. We can't move because of a sort of paralysis of mind, spirit, body. We can't seem to go on.

Indeed, it is true that we feel this way at times. But what that means is that we can't go back to where we were, to the way we were living and behaving. What has worked up till now no longer works. That it has broken down and come undone *is* bad news. But the good news is that if we admit that we have failed, if we recognize how foolhardy our efforts to keep on going are, then something else may come to be. Rising from the rubble of our own making, we might be invited to a new way of perceiving and being and acting. If we go back to the earlier ways of being and acting, we do so at our own peril. It is precisely those ways that have broken down before and will break down once again. We must seek and find a new way.

Breakdown, be it cultural or personal, allows for new possibility. It allows for deep hope in the future if it is accompanied by hope's counterpart — the admission of failure. The recognition of failure liberates us and moves us past the fixedness of a tightly held view of ourselves and of the world. In the throes of personal breakdown, we can look to alternative ways, often simpler and humbler ways of living. In the face of our massive cultural breakdown, we can look to persons and groups at the margins of society and church for a new sense of life's meaning and purpose. Those at the margins, both past and present, have usually not made it into the mainstream because their voices have been muted by those at the center. Their stories have been eclipsed by the governing myths by which we live. A myth such as "the American Dream" is empty of meaning for many persons and groups. Recognizing this emptiness can free us to hear anew and to receive gifts from other traditions.

One of our difficulties is that we are inclined to keep trying to hold up what is falling down and crumbling. We spend our energy trying to rebuild what is in a shambles, just like the person who keeps going back to earlier ways of behavior prior to an emotional or nervous breakdown. The sober fact is that it never really works, or at least not for long. We have to recognize the mess we are in and, rather than trying to fix it all up or patch together what has come apart, we would do better to wait and see what might come amidst the chaos. We can anticipate something else. We can hope.

More than anything else, hope is the retrieval of possibilities. And what may surprise us is that hope comes to us as a gift. Hope involves letting something that is not self-generated — not created by us — come into life. Given the enormity of the cultural collapse we face, we cannot hold it all together by ourselves. We must admit that we cannot keep it from falling apart. There is something very deep in us that refuses to admit failure. To admit failure and to open up to another way of doing things imply judgment, admitting that we are wrong. There is something deeply wrong with the way we have done it until now — in government, in family, in religious institutions, in religious life, in relationships between women and men, in our relationship to the earth and nonhuman life. We have failed. The "modern" worldview, whatever we might say about its strengths, has done untold damage.

In order to accept the gift being offered, even in the midst of the mess we are in, we must be ready to be judged. From a Christian perspective, we can say that God's intention for the world both now and to come is fundamentally at odds with our ways. The meaning and message of Jesus the Christ, his word and work, indeed his whole person, stand in marked contrast to our "modern" worldview. Unless we are willing to be judged, to submit our lives to the scrutiny of the Lordship of Christ and the power of the Holy Spirit, we cannot recognize and receive the possibility of perceiving and being in a new way. Like the truth expressed in the athlete's adage "No pain, no gain," it is true that hope is born in the admission of failure, in the acceptance of the judgment that our ways of being and acting need firm correction. There are others, indeed an Other, from whom we can learn.

If an admission of failure and a willingness to accept judgment are necessary for the rebirth of hope in our age, we also need a hefty dose of humility. Properly understood, humility is honesty. The humble person has a sober and realistic knowledge of where he or she stands, of who he or she is, of what their strengths and weaknesses might be. He does not pretend or put on airs; he does not stand above his situation in life, but right smack-dab in the midst of it. The humble person intends to be simple and straightforward. She admits her limits, the limits of those around her, and the limits of the world in which she lives. She faces facts. She admits what is true and doesn't try to defend the indefensible.

Alongside humility is poverty. In Christian theology, hope is linked to the beatitude of the poor in spirit. The person who is poor has open hands, with a natural disposition to welcome. No matter how little he has, he offers it. As he welcomes, receives, and offers, he finds yet more room, yet greater openness to what is to be given. Like emptiness, poverty opens us to some other possibility. Only when we are poor can we receive something not made of our own resources, from our own riches. This is altogether and utterly gift.

Hope is also linked in Christian theology to the gift of fear of the Lord. This might be better understood as filial fear, the fear of loss or separation that leads a child to cling to the parent. This kind of fear is what creates a necessary bond, a desiring for and clinging to the other. Fear in this sense is an indispensable part of hope, because hope looks to something that can still be lost because it is not yet fully attained.

When we see hope as gift, we are able to recognize
God's concrete interest in us. Scripture teaches that God
is most interested in us when we are poor and vulnerable.
Hope is indeed God's gift to the weak and the wounded.
When we are at our wits' end, powerless, in our darkest
hour, God can enter us and carry us forward. Through
the hope that comes as a gift of God's Spirit, we find
the strength to hold out for more, even in the most profound darkness. Through hope, we can let go, without
despairing or giving up.

Can We Hope Alone?

Of the many developments called "postmodern," perhaps
the one most helpful in thinking about a rebirth in hope
is the criticism today of individualism and self-sufficiency.
There is a new emphasis on the significance of relationship, specifically human relationships based on equality
and mutuality. This is important because hope always
looks beyond the self, recognizing the help that can come
from outside, from beyond, from another. Hope tells us
that there is an "other" who is important, in whom we
are anchored with every fiber of our being. Hope is always
exercised in relation to someone or something other than
the self. Hope depends on another, on others, on God. It
simply cannot be achieved alone. It searches and looks
to the outside world. Hope demands active waiting for
something beyond what one might achieve alone.

Hope stands a chance only in our relationship with

others and with God. This means that hope is always necessarily centered on a "we," not just an "I." While it is true that the self must remain the center of responsible action, since it is the "I" who acts hopefully, the hopeful person is one who recognizes that the self is not what is most important in the end. A person's thoughts, understandings, judgments, decisions, and actions must consider the other. We have a responsibility to the other. It is in the everyday face-to-face relation between myself and another that I might discover the still small voice that bids me to continue. When hope has been lost or betrayed or taken away, it is here that it begins again, with another person. It is within whatever limited arena of human activity that is ours, whatever small fire that has been given us to tend, that hope has its rebirth.

Here and now, even faced with meaninglessness, personal disaster, a seemingly never-ending cycle of breaking down and coming apart, we see the face of another, of a human person who demands a response from us. Even if there are spreading fissures running through our systems and institutions and organizations, there is always the face of a human person who looks at me and wants to know where I stand. The gazing, longing, penetrating face of another is not a system or an institution. It is a real person. It may be wounded and worn out and hollow, but this human face of the other brings me out of myself. The other demands a relationship and asks something of me.

What the other asks may be very simple: "Do no harm" or "Let me live." Or "Let life continue and flourish through the gift of your own life." It is in the human face of the other that I find a foothold for hope and the future. The future does not begin with some new world order or economic system or philosophy or theology. The future begins in this face-to-face relation, and so does hope. It begins as gift, beyond myself, offered in and through the face of the other.

God is welcomed in this face-to-face relation with the other. The trace of God is within me when I say "Here I am" in response to a plea from another. That other person draws me out of myself and toward something bigger. This trace of God stirs the hope that lies dormant through self-preoccupation, self-absorption, self-fixation. Hope is born not through a new vision of the future, but in doing what needs to be done for the other. When a person with concrete needs stands in front of me and pleads, "Where are you? Where do you stand?" I must listen to hear what she asks before I ask, "Who are you?" Even in our brief exchange, something may be given and received. Without seeking names or credentials, we must be open and responsible for the suffering of the other. Doing the good comes before settling the "big questions" about human nature, ultimate truth, or being. Once we reply, immediately, "Here I am, here I stand," hope begins. Hope lies in taking a first step toward the other, toward God.

F I V E

Through him you now have faith in God, who raised him from the dead and gave him glory for that very reason — so that you would have faith and hope in God. (1 Peter 1:21)

Speaking of Tongues

I had almost arrived. Having postponed this trip several times over the years, I had finally made it, or so I
thought. My flight to Paris and the train ride from Paris
to Compiègne was much like I had imagined. With my
never-really-spoken-before textbook French filed away in
my memory, I descended from the train at Compiègne
only to find that the last bus to Trosly-Breuil had left
an hour before. By that time I had been en route nearly
twenty-four hours, and I'm one of those people who can
never sleep on a plane. I searched for Trosly-Breuil on the
bus schedule posted in the train station and eventually
figured out that there would be no bus service to Trosly
until noon the following day. Not then part of the "over-
the-hill gang" of those past thirty, I decided to hitchhike.
Why hadn't someone told me that the buses didn't run in
the evening?

It was well past noon the next day when I finally woke
up from a long and strange sleep. I thought that the
strangeness might be coming from a curious smell that

filled the house. I just couldn't place it. Was it something cooking?

My hosts at l'Arche had given me a grass mat to sleep on. My mat was placed alongside several others in a large bedroom that drowned me in a sea of garish floral wallpaper. It actually hurt my eyes. There was no one on the other mats. They were probably ready to come home from work and here was the lazy American, just waking up. My mind had images of the evening before: hushed warm greetings during the night, the place somewhat like I had imagined, and an apology that the "cupboard" closes after supper so that slamming doors and rattling dishes won't wake up the household. It didn't much matter to me when I arrived since my hunger was eclipsed by my body's craving for sleep.

I was still exhausted from the long trip. The house seemed to be empty as I made my way down the stairs. It was quiet except for the wild wallpaper that screamed from every room. I heard voices but couldn't tell exactly where they came from. Haunted by the strange smell and hungry for anything at all, I began a hunt for the kitchen. And I mean a hunt. The location of the kitchen in this large, rambling French house wasn't obvious to me. I peeked in this door and that, hoping not to come upon the voices or, worse, to disturb a room full of occupants taking their afternoon siesta after a morning of hard work.

The kitchen was immense. On the range was a huge kettle nearly boiling over. And from it came the smell

that had greeted me on waking. I hadn't really intended
to "steal" food, but my hunger had become ravenous by
now, the kind that makes you dizzy. I neared the pot, very
self-conscious. This was someone else's kitchen, someone else's house, someone else's country. I decided that
I would just look at it and long for it until it made its way
to the supper table at six. When I remembered that supper time in France might not be before seven or even eight
o'clock, I panicked. There was a potholder on the counter.
My only thought as I grabbed it was to wonder what could
be the word for "potholder" in French.

As I lifted the lid I saw it rolling around in the boiling water. I knew what it was even though I had never
seen one before. It was long, thick, pimply, hideous looking, and I actually knew how to say it in French! My
high school French teacher had scolded us without end
about our pronunciation, about how we would never learn
la langue française unless we learned how to use our
langues, our tongues, in the right way. There it was. A
word I knew *en français* — *la langue.*

At the supper table that evening, although it was
smothered in a thin tomato sauce, the beef tongue
couldn't be disguised. As each plate was passed to the
center of the table to be served, I muttered something
about losing my appetite because of jet lag (another word
I didn't know in French!) and passed it up, politely I
hoped, nibbling on this and that. My dream had come
true. I was at table in the l'Arche community in France.
I was famished.

I had first heard about Jean Vanier and l'Arche in the late 1970s. L'Arche, French for the Ark, as in Noah's Ark, is the name of a worldwide community of the poor and wounded. Inspired by the beatitudes, it was founded by the Canadian Jean Vanier in France in 1964. Like the Ark from which the community took its name, Vanier's l'Arche was intended to be a place of refuge, diversity, and hope for both the mentally handicapped and those who live with them, the so-called "normal," the visibly strong and robust.

What drew me to the l'Arche community was Vanier's unique perspective on living in community with the handicapped. The l'Arche community does not exist just to properly care for the handicapped. At l'Arche the stronger people are not caregivers in the ordinary sense. Vanier's view is that the handicapped people, those who are weaker, form the core of the community, while the strong and robust are their "assistants." He believes that persons who are vastly different in terms of intellectual abilities and socio-economic backgrounds can live together and build lasting bonds of community. Probably his most important insight is that the handicapped have something valuable to teach others. This struck me as a perfect example of the quirky logic of the gospel: in dying we live, in losing our life we gain it, in weakness there is strength. The logic of l'Arche is that the seeds of the divine and the capacities of the human heart are found in weakness, not in strength.

Vanier's l'Arche communities spread to every continent and took the form of a worldwide movement. As a doctoral student in theology, my head filled with lofty speculations, I found Vanier's insights to be utterly true to the simple message of the gospel. Vanier and l'Arche symbolized for me the much-needed integration between good theology and the everyday living of the radical gospel message. If there was a way for me to put together head and heart, I thought, living in l'Arche could be the key.

Having latched on to the core ideas that motivate the l'Arche communities, I was eager for the opportunity to put them into practice. As with many things, this was easier said than done. Adjusting to strange dinner fare was only one small step in the much larger process of getting used to a totally different way of life. There was the hard work of lifting and washing and feeding and toileting and clothing others who needed help with the simplest tasks. There was the boredom of long days of tedious manual labor, something most graduate students are unused to. Doing menial tasks each day was beginning to get under my skin, as were some of the people whose shoulders I brushed up against day after day. Finally, there was the struggle to get along with people from different cultures who spoke different languages: we were French, Polish, British, Greek, Zairian, and American. Some days I longed for just one long afternoon to lounge at home with a thick novel in my hands. At l'Arche there was no time to read. The demands of community living required every inch and ounce of my energy.

I tried hard to live the l'Arche message of solidarity with the wounded and the weak. I put everything I had into it. But like most doctoral students and academic types, I began with my head. I thought about it and tried to figure out what it all meant the whole time I was trying to live it. My feet and hands and heart would never have followed my head had it not been for Luc.

My little community of ten lived in Breuil, Trosly's neighboring village. The community and its house were called La Nacelle, for the basket that holds the passengers in a hot air balloon. One of the things I loved most about La Nacelle was the opportunity to pray together in the evenings. When the dishes were done, everyone gathered in the living room. Those not in wheelchairs would sit cross-legged in a circle on the floor. In the center someone would place a lighted candle and a cross or an icon. We prayed to God, to Jesus, to Mary, sometimes using set prayers, but most often spontaneously from our hearts. There were prayers of petition for a parent or for an assistant leaving the community or for someone struggling with an illness. There would be prayers for someone on her birthday followed with a chorus of the French equivalent of "Happy Birthday." Usually some prayers would seek forgiveness for a misunderstanding or disagreement at the supper table. Inevitably, Eric, a core member who wasn't comfortable with group activities, would wander off to the corner of the room and enter his own contemplative zone after lighting up an after-dinner *Gitane* and puffing away.

One night it was my turn to read the scripture passage in French from the Bible the community had given me for my birthday the week before. After several months in the community, I still stumbled and searched through my mental French files to find the right words. Now I had to read aloud for the benefit of others. Thank God that it was not one of those readings about Hananiah, Azariah, or Mishael, the names we stumble over even in English. Although my relatively simple passage about the vine and the branches hadn't sounded so bad when I spoke it to myself in my own head, I was afraid. Community members were very patient with me in one-on-one conversation, but this was my first public performance!

Luc, a man roughly my own age, was seated across from me. He was the core member in our house who required the most care and attention. He had difficulty communicating with others because of his limited speech. During those months I struggled to understand what he was saying and often grew visibly impatient. Sometimes I would nod *"Oui,"* without a clue about what he had said, the way you might do with a child who babbles on while you've got something "important" to do. Yet, nearly always, even though you try not to hurt someone's feelings, sooner or later they catch on.

When I took up my Bible to begin reading, Luc seemed inattentive. He had grown accustomed to living in his own world, rocking and muttering and poking at himself here and there, waving his hands in the air and then pulling his palm toward his face as if to speak to it. I began to read, fumbling on every line, stuttering my way through, backing up and starting a word over, mispronouncing that beautiful language. Luc's gaze was suddenly riveted on me as consonants and vowels were voiced and gathered together in some approximation of a word. He seemed mesmerized. Somehow, Luc saw in my search for words his own deep and lifelong struggle to communicate. For those moments, I knew and felt his pain in the deepest kind of communion.

A few years later I received notice from the head of La Nacelle that Luc had died. I was sad because I knew his loss would be felt deeply at l'Arche, above all by the men and women at La Nacelle. But my own sadness was immense because I had also lost someone, someone who had taught me what I could not learn from books and what no one else at l'Arche had been able to teach me. Luc had shown me that the deepest communion is born of a shared vulnerability. In weakness we are born and in weakness we die. Although there are moments in between of strength and power and achievement, they pass. The constant throughout the life of each one of us is our absolute dependency on others, on God.

We who feel ourselves strong or clever or robust often desperately seek ways to avoid encounters with the handicapped, the seriously ill, the elderly or little children, those who manifest their vulnerability in explicit ways. Do they frighten us because we are petrified of the revelation of our own weakness and vulnerability? Our own limits? But our vulnerability cannot be avoided; it is written into the very being of who we are. We need the handicapped and the weak to teach us who we really are, to show us where our heart lies, buried beneath the layers of intelligence and our inordinate desire for competition and achievement. The heart in each one of us is a region of wound and weakness. This weakness is blessed because in it are found the seeds of the divine, the capacity to flourish in human relationships, the desire for authentic community.

So, in the end, the message of l'Arche entered my head, hands, feet, and heart. I have tried to live its wisdom even as my life has taken unexpected twists and turns. These days I often find myself in front of a classroom full of students who may have little interest in what I'm saying. Yet I try to let them know about the weakness and vulnerability of Jesus as the revelation of God's infinite mercy and compassion, and that this is the most important thing in life. Semester after semester, year by year they gaze at me, sometimes as uncomprehending as if I were speaking a foreign language. To them that's what it is. Most of them have not yet tasted life on their knees. They have not felt their lives come apart. Only those who have been deeply wounded through abuse or alcoholism or divorce or drug addiction, those who have been forced to look into the ruins of their lives, have any clue about what I am trying to say.

I used to be nervous before speaking in front of large crowds. Now I've gotten used to it, somewhat. It's not the number of people that unsettles me, but the look of the auditorium or — even worse — the ballroom where the crowd is assembled. The crystal chandeliers and red-carpeted hallways of the Hilton or the Hyatt provide a strange atmosphere for what I have to say. And a speaker must be able to effectively use the microphones and the complicated audiovisual equipment. The speaker is also expected to be "on," to entertain, to say something significant. (After all, the audience has paid good money for this!) You are encouraged to keep it lively, tell some jokes, give them a couple of good lines.

All the while I look desperately amidst the cacophonous clutter of my own making to see if there is just one person, just one listener who knows my language. I remember that room with the floral wallpaper, less garish because of the flickering of small votive lights against the faces of that tattered circle of friends at l'Arche. I see the flapping of those hands, the poking and picking at himself as Luc gazes fixedly at the palm of his own hand. And I remember the stillness as his eyes latch on to mine, seeing right through to my heart. I am in communion with him still, even now, whether it's a hotel ballroom, a parish hall or even a classroom. In this deepest communion I am able to see, if only for an instant, the desperate stuttering of each human heart as it struggles to speak — and to hear — a language of compassion and mercy.

Christ: The Ground of Hope

When Christians refer to Christ "our hope" or to "the hope of Christians," we don't refer so much to hoping itself but rather to the origin of our hope in God's promise or in the person of Jesus Christ. What does it mean when we say that Christ is the ground of hope, or that Christ gives hope? Do we indeed believe that Christ and the Christian tradition have anything to say to us in this day and age? My answer is solidly and emphatically "yes."

Hope is the theme of the entire Bible. Both testaments are laden with anticipation of some future good, be it the end of a flood, deliverance from slavery, or the coming of the Messiah. The Jewish community listened to its prophets and watched constantly for signs of the good to come. In both Hebrew and Christian scriptures, hope is ineluctably tied to membership in God's people. In both testaments, this hope is the hope of the *people*, not of this or that person. It was only much later that hope came to be seen and spoken of in terms of the individual. Fortunately, even today, given our preoccupation with individualism, with *my* rights and *my* needs, there are some theologians (often associated with liberation or political theology) who have recovered the collective, communal nature of hope. This understanding of the hope of a community or a people has often called attention to the meaning of redemption and salvation and to crucial social issues that lead to oppression and to despair.

The failure of our individualistic culture reminds us that we are intended to be part of communities and traditions and that we need others to live. Scripture shows us clearly that the Jewish and Christian faiths both affirm that individuals are part of a larger whole. We Christians are a covenant people whose identity is found in being and building the Body of Christ. This is why we say Christ is "our hope" and "we" put our hope in him. It is the Christ with us, in us, and for us who makes us a community.

The crumbling of the modern world also calls us to reevaluate our understanding of God's will. Many understandings of divine order and divine providence see God as a guarantor. Belief in God guarantees that things will work out for the best. God answers prayers by assuring good outcomes. In such a view, God's power is that of a divine monarch — dominating and absolute, a God who can solve all our problems. But when we look around us today, it can be difficult to see our lives unfolding according to a heavenly preordained plan. We experience life quite differently. What we actually experience is illness, accidents, randomness, suffering, diminishment and death, and much more.

Moments of healing and joy do break into our lives, as hope does through darkness, and belief in the midst of doubt. Even when there seems no precise cause in the natural order of things, there are fragmentary moments of joy and compassion. Gifts are given, something new is offered, and this is good news. But the good news is a promise of presence, of final fulfillment; it is *not* a guarantee that God is always "in charge," controlling the universe. God is not the God of unrestricted power to dominate and control by force, manipulating human life and history for noble purposes.

The Christian understanding of the importance of tradition, of community, and of hope without guarantees of predetermined, fixed outcomes can be good news for us. This may be unwelcome news for those who seek a free and easy ride down a spiritual superhighway, or for those whose spirituality is a purely private, individual pursuit. The Christian God is not part of a "do-it-yourself, fix-me-up plan." Many expressions of spirituality today, including some Christian spiritualities as well as those called "New Age," neglect the necessary place of community and the inevitability of suffering and negative experience.

Today Christian spirituality offers more good news. Prevailing understandings of God have crumbled, especially those in which God controls all things. We see the evidence around us every day. Our ache in the face of this loss — of what we thought we knew about God — calls us to cultivate deep reserves of trust and hope. We must strengthen our conviction that God's unfathomable fidelity is found in both promise and presence. God is trustworthy not because of unrestricted power to intervene and manipulate human affairs on our behalf; God is trustworthy because of a promise given and sustained in Christian communities throughout generations. These circles of memory and hope urge us on.

This loss of God as the divine commander affects every dimension of our lives. It demands that we allow God to come on God's own terms in ways we cannot predict or imagine or control. This is the moment to trust absolutely that the most compelling sign of God's presence and action in our lives is the stripping away of our images of God so that we might participate fully in the life of the living God. Our images cannot fully hold God. They limit God and they limit us. God is always ahead of us, over-spilling our closely held plans and our tightly knit ideas. This involves risk. We must accept losing our familiar and comforting images of God, becoming altogether and absolutely empty of them, so that the gift of God as Other can come to us on God's terms.

The Stirring of Christian Hope

Rising from the rubble of today, there are lives that stand as beacons. Their stories let us know that there is hope where none seemed to be. Sometimes there is no reasonable explanation why some find hope and others don't. In some it is deeply rooted, and others' grasp on it seems so very tenuous. In the words of American poet Emily Dickinson, hope is "the thing with feathers, that perches in the soul." You find hope by hoping.

When we are staggered by our failed plans or circumstances beyond our control, we must not look first and foremost for a God of guarantees. We must seek the One whose word is a promise of presence, but we must not seek any guarantees about how this presence will abide. This God has promised to be present to creation and active in history. Our problem is that we always want to be sure. We seek the sort of certainty demanded by the children of Israel in the wilderness. It was their need to know, to have a sign, that prompted Moses to take his staff and slam it against the rock (Exodus 17:1–7). Perhaps our human need to know is why so many signs of God's presence are sprinkled throughout both testaments. The followers of Jesus demanded signs. All four gospels recount stories of the scribes or Pharisees or Sadducees (or apostles) seeking signs, proof, guarantees that Jesus was the long-awaited Messiah, that expectations were being met, that there was a neat and tidy plan. But instead of fulfilling conventional certainties about God's plan of salvation for the chosen people, Jesus interrupted and disturbed. Jesus usually refused to give signs, demanding faith instead. And the promises offered by Christ flew in the face of tightly held expectations. Christ's very coming and his death on the cross were discontinuities with all that was judged to be God's way and work in the world.

Even amidst the ruins, many of which are of our own making, we can be buoyed up by the conviction that precisely in the midst of the movements and events that boggle and baffle us, God's presence abides. It calls us to vigorous engagement. It entails movement toward something or someone. It requires entrusting ourselves to a way, or making a way where none exists. This is Christian commitment, doing what we do every day with the one life we have and relinquishing guarantees so that we can risk. It means participating in a way of life grounded in the knowledge that beyond or beneath all deepest longings there is only one thing we ultimately hope for: union with the One whose heart is sought by our hearts.

Encounter with the Person of Christ

Christian hope is grounded in the person of Jesus Christ. It is in his call to us, in our encounter with him, and in the claim he makes upon us that the stirrings of hope begin. His request is not insignificant because he asks no less than our life. The encounter with Christ is truly an encounter with "the other." No matter how much he is like us and we share humanity with him, he is also altogether different from us. In the depth of his personhood he is divine. He calls us out of ourselves, toward something or someone not of our own making.

In his otherness, Christ judges our ways of perceiving and being in the world. In that face-to-face relation I come to know that person I have not yet become, that person I am called and hope to be. The encounter with Jesus Christ leaves a trace in me. It gives me a hunch about how to move toward the future and about what kind of future is worthy of my hope.

When we are asked in this face-to-face encounter,

"Where are you? Where do you stand?" we must respond
that we stand for Christ, in Christ. I do not stand first
and foremost on this or that philosophy or theology, or for
these or those principles or values. The ground in which
my life is anchored is Christ. That is where I stand and
that is enough. From this recognition and acceptance, the
rest follows.

We might have only traces, but they are sufficient. Although Christ has gone before us, the cross remains and
our Christian life is lived in the shadow of the cross. It
gives us a clue about the cost of Christ's claim on us, yet
hints also of new life. Suffering and death are *not* the final
word. At the foot of the cross, Mary and John were dev-
astated by their loss, yet their despair gave rise to hope.
They made their way between darkness and light. The
wisdom of the cross is the realization that suffering and
loss touch every life. But the very stuff of life, every inch
and ounce of it, including suffering and loss, has been
embraced by God in Christ.

To Lament Is to Hope

These changing perspectives invite new experiences and
expressions of life and of prayer. Above all, the loss of our
familiar image of God the guarantor, the one who calls
all the shots, must be named for what it is. A familiar,
controlling God might be what we want, but it is not what
we were promised and it is not what is. The loss must

be faced, and the absence of the familiar grieved. This we need to lament.

Lamentation of loss has its place in Christian life and prayer. Lamentation is not endless moaning. To lament is to cry out to God in anguish and in hope, and this makes lamentation a bold act of faith. Our crying out to God beyond all images and concepts makes room for the divine presence to break through in human life, history, world, and church. To pray in our day is to lean into the ache of absence rather than to retreat to the familiar pattern of giving lip service to a God who formerly was counted on to intervene in human affairs. But no longer.

Only when the heart knows the ache of absence do the reserves of hope that dwell there rise up in unrelenting thanksgiving. It is only in the ache of Christ's dying that life anew gives cause for awe and wonder. Only when the depth of absence is lived long and lovingly can the heart awaken to Christ's constant coming. It is a perfect act of praise for us to keep on in the hope that all is not chaos. In the shadow of our loss, in the shadow of the cross, we give thanks and praise to the living God whose presence is anticipated. And our hope begins. Again.

S I X

*For in hope we were saved. Now hope that
sees for itself is not hope. For who hopes for
what one sees? But if we hope for what we do
not see, we wait with endurance.*

(Romans 8:24–25)

Doxology in Darkness

"She is just about as old as the year we're in." This is how Mother would help us kids remember our grandmother's age. "She was born on August 19, 1899. Now how old does that make her?" My sister, Maureen, and I would count up the years, always a bit unsure if we were getting it right. Never good at math, I remember protesting that it would have been so much easier had she been born in 1900, " 'cause then she'd be sixty in 1960, and sixty-one in 1961." The next question inevitably followed: "Who's older, Nanny or Aunt Agnes?" My grandmother Mary Ann and her twin sister, Agnes, never told us. It's as if one did not want to embarrass the other by letting the cat out of the bag. Because our Nan colored her hair while our Aunt Agnes, her twin, let hers go white, my sister and I were convinced that our grandmother was younger. Her buoyancy and laughter helped.

Nan "came out" to America while still a young woman. Born in High Glen in County Donegal in the northwest-ernmost corner of Ireland, she left that rugged place with its dark hills because there seemed to be no future for her there. Leaving took a kind of courage that many of my generation seem to know little about. Back then the Irish called the boats sailing to America "coffin ships." Those who set sail were as good as dead to their families and friends. If, indeed, they made it to the distant shore, it was more than likely that they would never be seen again by those at home.

My cousin Sadie tells about the "convoy" that sent Nan off to America. The cottage's earthen floor had been pounded by hours of dancing through the night to the music of fiddle, tin whistle, and accordion ("a-cordjeen" in Donegal). The house was still filled to overflowing when morning light came. Sadie's voice is soft as she tells of the goodbye. Everyone followed Mary Ann Boyce to the end of the road. In the still darkness of that morning, she gripped her father. Sadie says that Mary Ann's companions had to tear her away from him lest she miss the boat. "It's the howling and wailing from out of the soul of her that I remember," Sadie says. Her father lingered for hours, straining to glimpse the coffin carrying his daughter away from him.

She had learned early on to work very hard. So poor was her family that they could not afford to keep her at home, so she had been hired out as a farm hand. She cherished the rare times she could be at home with the other Boyces. In Philadelphia, the "City of Brotherly Love," there was plenty of hard work for her. First, she worked as a housekeeper in Catholic rectories and then later as a maid for "rich ladies." One of the ladies was so rich, Nan said, that she took her to their plantation in Aiken, South Carolina, to care for her children. Whatever Nan earned, she saved and sent it back home to High Glen so that her twin sister, Agnes, could also come out to America.

"No one believes they're twins," everyone in the family would say. One fair, the other dark. One serious, the other so much fun. One so nice, devout, religious, the other headstrong and fiercely independent. But over the years I learned that this was a way of talking around deeper and more painful differences. Aunt Agnes had a good turn of luck after arriving in America; Nan had a hard row to hoe — at every turn. Agnes married a fine Irishman from Ireland's County Monaghan who cared for her and provided for her and for their children. Aunt Agnes and Uncle Pete "made it" in America.

Nan also married an Irishman, but it didn't work out. She was left alone in an Irish Catholic ghetto in West Philadelphia, with two children. "The church is against divorce," she always said flatly, so she carried the burden of rearing Peggie and Jimmy alone. It's different now, but in her day she was an enigma — a single mother of two children in a Catholic enclave. Everyone knew that she was without her man, but she never stopped wearing her wedding band. She was always Mrs. McCauley.

Mother says often that no matter how hard the times, Nan always saw to it that there was a small piece of meat on the table for the two children, except on Fridays, of course, and then it was fish. Meat on the table in those days signified some measure of stability, a small sign of prosperity. To Nan it meant that she was able to provide for her children even in the worst of times.

I always remember her working or getting ready to go to work. Most weekends when she wasn't working she came to our house. I loved having her there. I wanted her to live with us — permanently. She was the only grandparent I had, and I was her favorite. She always had a dime to give me for a Pepsi. In later years, to my mother's dismay, she'd come into our house, sit down with her huge pocketbook, and then call me over with the glad tidings: "Here's a quarter; go buy yourself a packet of cigarettes."

One Sunday afternoon we crouched on the living room floor after supper, I in my teens and she in her sixties. We were shooting marbles. Without a hint of warning, she piped up in her thickly buckled Ulster brogue: "I married him because I wanted to cook for him and give him a home." "Who?" I asked. "Your grandfather. You're getting older now and so I thought you should know." I had wondered, but never asked. It was the first and last word I ever heard from her on that subject, but others talked. They said he was cursed with the "Irish virus." He took her earnings as well as his own and spent the money on drink. When he began taking things from the children so he could buy a shot of whiskey, she gave him his walking papers.

She took great pride in dressing in "the whole style." Though she had very little, she wanted to look sharp and "modren." When she went to a party or to a dance she liked dresses with "seegrins" (read sequins). When I was in my early teens and visited Ireland with her, all the family spoke of "what a lovely beauty she had on her when she was young." In singing her praises there was always a hint of remorse that her life had turned tragic in America.

Nan lived down the block from my school, Most Blessed Sacrament. She worked the odd shift, from four in the afternoon till midnight, at a factory in North Philadelphia. From MBS school I would go to her house on Regent Street for lunch Monday through Friday. Mother always said that it would be easier all around if I had lunch at Nanny's. "It brightens up her day. It gives her something to do besides work all the time." I liked going there, though I remember the house was so dark inside, even at midday. But she made wonderful soup. I can still taste her cake and hear the echoes of her telling how many eggs had gone into it. And we always drank tea — real tea leaves, of course — with lots of milk. There was no sugar in the tea. That was only for the rich, she said.

While I ate lunch in the kitchen, she often sat in the living room — dark or dimly lit. "The electric costs money. We can't afford to live like the ascendancy with lights burning through the house night and day," she'd say. She would think, or ponder, or gaze, or brood. I was never sure what it was. Sometimes I would hear her whispering, but could never quite make it out. When I left she would see me to the door and she'd sprinkle me with holy water from the small font nailed to the wall near the front door. Her farewell bidding never changed: "Thanks for comin' in."

Poor eyesight and little education meant she couldn't read well, but she listened to the news on the radio from time to time. She watched TV at our house, but she had no use for it when she was alone. By herself, in her dimly lit front room, she would sit for hours on end going over it all in her head. When she went to bed at night at our house she could be heard whispering long into the night. Here and there, in the midst of the half-audible rattling in between her insomnia and slim minutes of dozing, I often caught words of her prayers in her native Gaelic.

I took every chance I could to be around her. Usually confined to the city, she loved going for a ride in the country, "away out in the wilderness." She loved being driven, accustomed as she was to making her way through the city by trolley and subway. Getting my driver's license meant that I could treat her to a ride, and she would buy me a cup of coffee somewhere on the road. At home it was buckets of tea, but at a restaurant or after Sunday supper at our house we had coffee with lots of cream and way too much sugar.

Our times together grew less frequent as I moved on to college and graduate school. She continued to work well beyond the age of retirement, fooling employers about her age and amazing co-workers with her strength and endurance. "Mrs. McCauley works harder than any of the others, and at her age!" her manager boasted.

Nan continued to root for me. Whatever I did was just

fine with her. After I finished college, when I was searching to find my way, she assured me: "Whatever you do you'll be good at. But nothin's as good as a priest." Undoubtedly she had a hidden hope for me. Nonetheless, she continued to delight in my life and in the unfolding of a future more promising than she could have imagined for herself, even though it began to take a turn different from what she might have hoped.

The change happened rather unexpectedly and quickly. On her birthday in August she seemed as always. "No change on her," Mother remarked gratefully. Signs of age, to be sure, but nothing dramatic. By the onset of autumn, though, there were telltale signs. Mother called each day, and, for the first time in memory, there would be no answer at Nan's house. On her unannounced visits, Mother would be greeted reluctantly and sheepishly from behind closed curtains and bolted door.

In a matter of weeks it was clear that she had indeed changed. She was "acting crazy." One day when we found her at the bottom of the stairs, pinned down by a door she was singlehandedly trying to unhinge for reasons unknown, it was clear there was no choice. Nan was coming to live with us. My dream had come true, but in a way I had not anticipated. I was long gone from my childhood home, and Nan no longer was herself.

She had always seemed to favor boys. My Uncle Jimmy was incapable of any wrongdoing in her eyes; the same was true for me. My mother, Peggie, much like Nan herself, was headstrong, a survivor, fiercely independent. No surprise then that there were tensions between mother and daughter long before it became fashionable to examine the dynamics of mother-daughter relationships. But Mother was the elder child, and it seemed the right thing for her to care for Nan. During nearly ten years of constant care, much of Nan's stubborn streak remained and often took the form of defiance in the face of any request for cooperation. And then there was also the part about not being able to teach an "old dog new tricks." Some attributed the increasingly bizarre behavior to hardening of the arteries to the brain and others used the generic label "dementia," which I abhorred. We wondered whether it was a standard case of the onset of senility. Then there was talk of the beginnings of Alzheimer's disease.

Nearly ten years passed before Mother asked for some relief. Then my Uncle Jimmy and his wife, Pat, took Nan into their home, along with Pat's aging father. Before long he died, and Nan's condition worsened. Peggie and Jimmy then faced the heartrending decision of turning their mother over to the constant care of a nursing home. There seemed no other choice. They had done everything they were capable of doing.

I don't get back to Philadelphia very often. There are the occasional trips for holidays, for weddings, for funerals. But I never go home without going to spend some time with my Nan.

Most often she sits in her wheelchair in the solarium, surrounded by other white-headed ladies who ponder, or brood, or doze and drool, or wail in their pain. She usually has someone else's clothes on. Hard as we tried to keep her clothes from getting mixed up in the laundry, we never quite managed. We're not the only ones. All the ladies seem to be wearing flowery printed dusters too big or too small for them but all seemingly cut from the same cloth and the same pattern. And so is their hair: blunt cut, stark white. The faces begin to look all the same, too. No longer dressed in "the whole style" and brightened by her signature auburn rinse, I have a tough time picking her out from this crowd of look-alikes. From afar, I spot her. I want to watch her from a distance, to know how she lives in this world of endless waiting. My whole being, already soaked through with the smell of urine-dowsed diapers, aches for her. I wonder if she'll still know me.

I bend down so that I can look into her eyes, so that she can see me. "Hi, Nan. It's Michael." She looks toward me with no glimmer of recognition. "Do you know me?" Faintly, "No." "I'm your grandson Michael. Do you know me?" Finally, in a deep and throaty groan she nods, "Michael." Our conversation ends. I take her hand and put it to my cheek. She takes my hand and touches it, rubs it, pressing it to herself time and again. I assure her, "Peggie's fine. She's working and taking care of herself now that Eddie's dead. You know Eddie, my dad, is gone five years now. You remember Eddie. Sure you do. But Peggie's okay now. And so's Maureen and the boys. And Jimmy and Pat and the kids. We're all okay." I try

to fill the great gaps of silence. "How are you, Nan?" She
looks to me helplessly as I strain to decipher: "Not good.
I have no clothes. I can't do nothin'."

I want to tell her so much, but I cannot find a way. My
feelings are too big. They stumble in finding a way to my
lips. The words of my heart come to a halt as she looks
into me and wonders. I'm not sure she really hears me. I
don't know what she takes in.

Her brand of Irish was never much for "plusterin'."
That's Irish for being a bit too demonstrative, showing a
bit too much tenderness and affection. But I gaze into that
face and take those hands and smile as my tears begin to
blind me. My heart wants to pound the darkness till it
bleeds light.

From within this heart of mine springs the deepest
kind of wordlessness, the only language of sadness and
lament, and of praise and thanks for this strong and stubborn life, for this courage, for this indomitable spirit that
even now in this utter darkness simply refuses to quit. I
take the wrinkled flesh of her hands in my hands, those
hands that worked and sacrificed without end to make a
better life for her children, her grandchildren and great-
grandchildren. Her finger is ringless, too thin even for her
precious wedding band. I want to cradle her body so frail
and broken by hard work, the likes of which I've never
known.

There is a light that lets us see each other. I lift my
eyes and bless God for a life so broken and frail at its
end, a life in which there seems no hope, no light. For

her there is usually only the darkness. Yet from the wells
of my soul comes a shimmering hope stirred on by the
memory of her Irish prayers. Words find their way to my
lips, whether to Nan or to God, I do not know: "In you,
day and darkness are bright."

She ponders, she worries, she whispers. The light in
my mind's eye sees her in her house on Regent Street,
in that dark, dimly lit room. She's looking after me,
putting "half a dozen eggs in that cake," and then sitting
down to rest before getting me back to school and herself off to work. I also hear the rattling, chattering, faint
echoes of her prayers for me spoken in the language of her
childhood.

If you cannot pray now, my Nanny, let my lips carry
your words to the God who seemed so far from you
through a life so troubled and broken. Never did you stop
raising your voice in prayer. And now that your life is at
its end and you are held somewhere between us and the
God you never abandoned, your staying with us still is a
testimony to the light, even in your darkness.

I have to tear myself away from her. Each time I think it
may be the last. I stand to leave her and imagine the small
holy water font at the door on Regent Street. Gently, I put
my thumb on her forehead, marking her with the sign of
Christ's cross. And each time she answers, "Thanks for
comin' in."

Conclusion

Memory stirs hope. When we are able to look back over the years and across the miles, we see that it is precisely at our most vulnerable point that God enters our lives. We see that the seeds of the divine and the capacities of the human heart are found in weakness, not in strength. There *is* reason for hoping. It is precisely when we are at our limits that hope begins. We can draw confidence from knowing that hope can find a home and room to grow in our own painful emptiness and utter poverty.

In this little book on hope, I have tried to express my understanding of the loss and recovery of hope in a very dark age. To do this, I have woven together poetry, snippets of theological insight, and personal stories springing from my Irish storyteller's heart. Poem and story move us from feeling and affect toward greater understanding. As we become aware, theological concepts can then provide a framework for understanding more fully this mysterious reality called "hope," that which comes only as a gift from God.

A good deal has changed since this book took seed several years ago. Our age has grown even darker and seemingly even more hopeless. At the same time, the Catholic church prepares for the great Jubilee year 2000 through prayer and reflection on the persons of the Trinity, as well as on the virtues of faith, hope, and charity.

Indeed, this is the year of hope, its season, its moment. Hope is not waiting for the time when things seem just a little brighter. Hope begins now, by hoping.

In memory's eye I look long and lovingly at those people whose stories I have told here. Each one continues on the way, providing a glimmer of light amidst the ruins and the rubble of our age. There have been slips and falls along the way, but no one has turned back or completely let go. Some have picked up and moved on. Others have had to begin again, and yet again.

My beloved grandmother is now radiant with the brilliance of Christ in glory. Together with all those who have gone before us, she waits for those whom she loved to join her. She hopes, too. Even as she awaits the fullness of resurrection, she hopes and will hope for all eternity.

In the end, three things last — faith, hope, and love. Hope endures and does not end. It is God's gift, God's very life in us eternally. The gift expresses the life of the giver, God's life. God continually gives the gift of hope and yet is never empty of it. God also continues in hope by hoping. Even now, God anticipates and waits. God's coming in flesh waited for the free response of Mary of Nazareth. Her "yes," her hope that God's promise would be fulfilled, changed everything. Likewise, God waits for our "yes." God hopes in us, for us, with us. This is the reason for the hope that lives within us. Yes, even when we cannot see the road ahead of us because the candle has gone out and we are in utter darkness, the lines of our life's story can still be written out in hope.